Readings: A New Biblical Commentary

General Editor
John Jarick

1 TIMOTHY

Further titles in the Readings: A New Biblical Commentary Series

1 TIMOTHY

Deborah Krause

T&T CLARK INTERNATIONAL
A Continuum imprint
LONDON • NEW YORK

Published by T&T Clark International
A Continuum imprint
The Tower Building, 11 York Road, London SE1 7NX
15 East 26th Street, Suite 1703, New York, NY 10010

www.tandtclark.com

British Library Cataloguing-in-Publication Data
A catalogue record for this book is available from the British Library

Typeset by Data Standards Ltd, Frome, Somerset BA11 1RE
Printed on acid-free paper in Great Britain by Cromwell Press

ISBN   0-567-08159-1 (hardback)
       0-567-08169-9 (paperback)

To Katherine Hawker and Jeanne W.S. Smith

Periechomenai tas oikias ... lalousai ta me deonta
1 Timothy 5.13

Contents

Non-Canonical Abbreviations

1 QS	*The Community Scroll* (Dead Sea Scrolls)
AP	*Acts of Paul*
BAGD	*A Greek-English Lexicon of the New Testament and Other Early Christian Literature*, 2nd edn (Chicago: University of Chicago Press, 1979)
BCE	Before Common Era (same dates as BC)
CE	Common Era (same dates as AD)
Did	*Didache*
GM	*Gospel of Mary*
KJV	King James Version
LXX	Septuagint
NRSV	New Revised Standard Version
PE	Pastoral Epistles (1 and 2 Timothy and Titus)
Pol	*Polycarp to the Philippians*
RSV	Revised Standard Version

Preface

Several years ago I received a letter. Along with greetings and other standard elements of the contemporary genre of letters, this letter contained an invitation. The invitation was to write a commentary for Sheffield Academic Press (now T&T Clark) for their 'Readings' series of biblical commentaries. Upon seeing that most of what I would have considered 'plum' assignments were taken (e.g. Matthew, Mark, Luke, John, most of Paul's writings, etc.) I noted that there was a little letter, oft maligned, that remained unassigned. That letter was 1 Timothy. A challenging relationship was born.

The prospect of writing a definitive commentary on 1 Timothy was daunting. The idea that the commentary, as a genre, offers an exhaustive exploration of the text's meaning seemed to be a leviathan task. In addition, as repositories of information about given texts, there are many published critical commentaries on 1 Timothy that contain detailed historical information about the text's origins and contents. I knew that I could not supplant or even significantly supplement the recent rigorous historical and literary analyses of commentaries on 1 Timothy by Collins, Bassler, Donelson, Dunn, and Quinn and Wacker.

The theme title for this commentary series intrigued me, however: 'Readings'. A reading, unlike a commentary, does not necessarily have to endure, I thought. A reading is more of a 'go through' or a 'take' on something than a definitive and exhaustive treatment of it. While I may not have much more philological insight to add to the interpretation of 1 Timothy, I definitely have a 'take' on the text.

This commentary is guided by the awareness that every reading of 1 Timothy, or any other text, is a 'take' on the text from a particular perspective. Indeed, even commentaries that assume the posture of comprehensive analyses of the text represent particular perspectives and biases. In this sense, the present work does not stand as an independent statement on *the* meaning of 1 Timothy, but offers a reading of the text of this letter that attends to what the text has meant and is meaning in different ways. It is a peculiar commentary, one that not merely interprets the text of 1 Timothy, but also interprets other texts. From editorial columns about murdering mothers to contemporary ecclesiastical manuals, from slave castles of Ghana, West Africa to states' rights debates in the Southern United States about use of the Confederate flag, this commentary represents a reading of many readings of 1 Timothy.

One might well ask: 'all this from such a little letter?' That is another aspect of 1 Timothy's power as a text. Its canonical placement gives this little letter power to speak for Paul, for 'the church,' and for God. With its polemical rhetoric against 'other teachings' and its calls to protect the 'strong words' of Jesus Christ the letter seems to bear tremendous self-consciousness about its official presentation of the traditions of the church. This little letter, along with 2 Timothy and Titus (together the 'Pastoral Epistles'), functions as a construing of the entire Pauline tradition of letters toward the goal of a particular vision of the church. While these letters pose as personal communication between Paul and Timothy and Titus they are driven to address not particular ecclesial dilemmas and crises, but rather the church, its beliefs and its practices in a more general way. In this sense, 1 Timothy, 2 Timothy and Titus are not only pseudepigraphical in their authorship and receivership, they are 'pseudo-epistolary' - meaning they assume the form of letters while doing the work of more general ecclesiastical teaching. 1 Timothy dresses as a little letter, but it has always functioned as a powerful statement about the purpose and nature of the church in the world.

The power of 1 Timothy to define the Pauline legacy is a power based within the power of words. It is a rhetorical power. This commentary reads 1 Timothy as a rhetorical construction that seeks to shape thinking about who Paul is and what the church is. In fact the defining aspect of this commentary on 1 Timothy is its attention to how the letter writer engages words and contends with words of his opponents. Rather than taking the letter writer at his word about Paul and the church, this commentary seeks to explore his words to understand better the rhetorical context within which he wrote, and to hear and appreciate the words of those whom the letter writer seeks to silence and disparage as 'outside' of the true faith and 'other' than the true church.

For the past few years as I have read, researched and written on 1 Timothy, I have been filled with ambivalence about the company I have been keeping. Reading 1 Timothy as a work of ancient pseudepigrapha I have been aware of an irony within the letter writer's rhetoric. The letter writer pretends to 'stand in' for the 'real' Paul. I am not sure who the real Paul was, but I know that all claims to authenticity are usually claims to power of some sort. They are attempts to assert the genuine and true over the 'fake'. The letter writer is pulling a power play. He demands what is true, and expects what is 'right' while he proposes to be someone he is not.

I have read and appreciate arguments that the letter writer writes in a context in which pseudepigraphy was a regular practice for schools of thought perpetuating the traditions of revered figures. I understand that his posing as Paul may represent the Platonic ethical concept of the 'good lie' that commits a small deception in pursuit of a greater good. In light of the particular claims of his letter and their reach in influencing the social reality of the church and the world, however, I have been forced to ask 'good for whom?' Keeping company with this writer has not always been a positive experience.

Nor has it been, however, entirely negative. As a 'stand in' for Paul, I have found myself sympathizing with the writer's predicament. The late first and early second centuries were tumultuous times for interpreters of the Christian tradition. The tradition was in the process of being established. Its canons were being set. Such liminal and defining times often make us pine for what is authentic and original. They can drive us to assert our perspective of the truth on the foundation of what we claim to be original. In a sense this perspective has given me more empathy for the writer of 1 Timothy. I understand his letters as his 'take' on Paul. Their elevation to canonical status is what has made them so defining. In and of themselves they are a 'reading' of Paul's gospel for the church that the Pastoral Epistle writer hopes to administrate and lead. As a 'reading' of Paul the letters are much less monolithic and threatening. They are a perspective to be heard and argued with. So in this commentary I venture forth with my particular reading of the Pastoral Epistle writer's 'reading' of Paul in 1 Timothy.

Since I have started on this project many friends, colleagues and acquaintances who know my feminist politics have questioned my choice to write a commentary on 1 Timothy. I assure them that far from an apologetic treatment of the text, I engage the letter's rhetoric critically and attempt to unmask its assumptions and constructions. While that is true, they pose a fair question. Why bother? As one who teaches in a theological seminary connected with the liberal tradition of the United Church of Christ and who is ordained within a moderate theological tradition of the Presbyterian Church, USA, I do not regularly have to encounter 1 Timothy's decrees that women should be silent and not have authority over men (1 Timothy 2.12), or that slaves should be submissive to their masters (1 Timothy 6.1-2). In my work for justice in my church and community I tend to encounter sexism and racism in the more subtle (and unfortunately more palatable) rhetorical forms. Why engage this antiquated relic and stir up these messages of ecclesial and social repression?

My answer to these questions is grounded in my interpretation of 1 Timothy as a rhetorical construction within a larger ecclesial and social debate. I understand 1 Timothy as one voice within a larger argument (found both between the lines of the Pastoral Epistles themselves, and in extracanonical Christian texts) about the nature of the church and its place in the world. In this sense, the study of 1 Timothy offers the opportunity to study the practice of Christian rhetoric in all of its multivocality and multivalence. In my teaching as a professor in a theological seminary training women and men for ordained Christian ministries I have found this project of study to be most appropriate for their formation as interpreters and practitioners of Christian rhetoric. In studying 1 Timothy and other texts as 'readings' of the Pauline tradition within a larger argument about the nature of the church in the world, students have the opportunity to become aware of their own ways of 'reading' tradition and understanding the 'readings' of others. Toward this end, out of my study of 1 Timothy I have designed a course entitled 'Following Paul' which explores the church in its interpretation of and rhetorical engagement with Paul's letters and legend in the late first and early second centuries CE. In this course the Pastoral Epistles, along with Ephesians and Colossians, the Acts of Paul, Marcion, the Gnostics and others are studied in terms of the different ways they each sought to follow Paul (see Appendix 1). The course, like as this commentary, seeks to appreciate the diversity of interpretations that arose out of following Paul, and engages these different interpretations of Paul as a way to understand the diversity of the church both historically and contemporarily.

In many ways the project of researching and writing this commentary has been one of contending with the Pastoral Epistle writer, but also with larger questions of what it means to honour tradition, what the church is and how the church orders its life in the world. While many of my students and I may understand the church differently to the writer of 1 Timothy, we all struggle with the problem of what it means to claim as authoritative the revelation of one who is dead and gone, and who leaves behind fragmentary and idiosyncratic letters as the source of his wisdom. In this perspective, the rhetoric of 1 Timothy becomes less 'other' to us, and our posture toward the letter writer becomes less antagonistic.

Rather than an enemy, I like to think of the writer of 1 Timothy as a distant Great Uncle. While he may be strange and even creepy, he is a member of the family and one with whom I need to learn to converse. If I deny my relationship with him I miss an opportunity to better understand who I am and what it is that I believe. Such a posture in relation to traditions such as 1 Timothy (be they in ancient or contemporary contexts) offers us a more modest and honest place from which to practise our own Christian rhetoric.

In the time of completing this 'reading' of 1 Timothy I have been indebted to many people. I have already mentioned my students in the 'Following Paul' seminar I teach at Eden Theological Seminary in St Louis, Missouri, USA. In the two semesters in which I have taught this course the students read carefully in primary texts of the first and second century CE and provided insights and criticisms that were generative for my own thinking and writing. In addition students who have participated in my seminars on Feminist and Womanist Biblical Interpretation have read 1 Timothy (along with many other texts) and brought their passion, imagination, and courage with them. In particular Rev. January Kiefer and Rev. Patricia Talton were, as Teaching Assistants, helpful in their feedback about my approach to the text. An appendix of a liturgical reading entitled 'The 'Silenced' Women of 1 Timothy 2:8-15' is included at the end of this book. It represents one piece of the fruit of critical and imaginative biblical interpretation from this course (see Appendix 2).

The Board of Directors of Eden Seminary offers a generous sabbatical policy that provided time away from teaching to do research and writing. My colleagues on the seminary faculty have been an encouragement and a support throughout this project. My Deans, John Bracke and now Joretta Marshall, have provided institutional support and emotional encouragement. In addition, Damayanthi Niles, Stephen J. Patterson, John W. Riggs, and Marcia Robinson (now of Syracuse University) have provided valuable guidance and friendship during these years. Likewise, colleagues in other places have heard my 'take' on Timothy, challenged me and supported me. I was privileged to read a paper on the Pastoral Epistles in the New Historicism Consultation of the Society of Biblical Literature, where I received helpful critiques on my perspectives. I am indebted to Robert Goss of Webster University with whom I have written on the Pastoral Epistles. Timothy K. Beal of Case Western Reserve University has been a motivating colleague, a kind critic, and a good friend.

The staff and editors of Sheffield Academic Press have been supportive and helpful during this project. Lorraine Bottomley graciously kept me updated of deadlines and offered answers to questions about style and format. John Jarick, the series editor, has been gracious about my missed deadlines and always encouraging toward the goal of completing the project. In addition the staff and editors of Continuum in the UK have been of great help. In particular I would like to thank Sylvia Marson, Pendleton Campbell, and Nick Fawcett for their careful work. In St Louis, my student and editorial assistant Dori Hudson has carefully read the complete manuscript of the commentary and judiciously applied her pen to overdrawn sentences, made requests for clarifications and corrected my grammar. I am in her debt for a greatly improved manuscript.

Throughout this commentary I challenge the writer of 1 Timothy that his vision of the church is merely one way the church can be imagined. The writings of the non-canonical *Acts* (such as the *Acts of Paul and Thecla*) helped to expand my canonically shaped horizons to see that the church was variously (heterodoxically) ordered when 1 Timothy was written. However, the various experiences I have had in my own church membership have most emboldened me to challenge the social hierarchies of 1 Timothy. In particular the congregation of Oakhurst Presbyterian Church in Decatur, Georgia, and the congregations of Evangelical United Church of Christ, Webster Groves and First Presbyterian Church, St Louis have provided communities in which my spirit and imagination have been nurtured for social justice and cooperative ministry among women, men and children. These places in their worship, mission and fellowship have sustained me as I have argued with the writer of 1 Timothy. They have encouraged me to understand that 'other ways' of being church can be understood as the diversity of God's revelation as much as deviant communities of lost souls destined for destruction. For me these churches have been 'bulwarks of the truth', not in the letter writer's sense of protecting the tradition, but in the sense of sustaining a conversation in which diversity of thought and experience is seen as a virtue rather than a vice.

I owe the greatest thanks to those who are in my household: Isabel, Rebekah Jane and Bill. At times during the past few years as the household has fallen down around us, laundry piling up and dishes in the sink, I have wondered if the letter writer's demands of social hierarchy for the good of order have not had their place. In the midst of our daily struggle to live our professional and personal lives while caring for and enjoying children I have wondered if the letter writer might see me as a victim of one of his opponents who in 2 Timothy 3.6 he describes as those who 'barge into houses and capture weak women ... who will study with anybody and are never able to come to the knowledge of truth' (NRSV). Perhaps I should not have been such an eager student of the feminist critique of patriarchy. Perhaps if my family and I had structured our household as the letter writer imagines we would live in order and avoid much chaos. Yet with my family in our house, as difficult as it has been at times, there is a promise of something more than order, a promise of what the letter writer so disparagingly calls 'other ways'. For that promise, and the privilege to pursue its joy and freedom with them, I do thank and bless all those who are in my house.

Finally, as this commentary attends primarily to issues of speech and power, in particular women's speech, I thank my friends Katy Hawker and Jeanne Smith with whom I have learned much about the double-edged power of talk both to resist situations of oppression and to create opportunities for freedom. For 'gadding about from house to house' with me, and for 'saying what they should not' (1 Timothy 5.13), I thank them. It is to our friendship and our ongoing conversation that I dedicate this book.

Introduction to Reading 1 Timothy

> These things, brethren, I write to you concerning righteousness, not
> at my own instance, but because you first invited me. For neither am
> I, nor is any other like me, able to follow the wisdom of the blessed
> and glorious Paul, who when he was among you in the presence of
> the men of that time taught accurately and stedfastly [*sic*] the word of
> truth, and also when he was absent wrote letters to you, from the
> study of which you will be able to build yourselves up into the faith
> given you.
>
> *Pol.* 3.1, trans. Kirsopp Lake, Loeb Classics, 1912

> Therefore, beloved, since you wait for these, be zealous to be found
> by him without spot or blemish, and at peace. And count the
> forbearance of our Lord as salvation. So also our beloved brother Paul
> wrote to you according to the wisdom given him, speaking of this as
> he does in his letters. There are some things in them hard to
> understand, which the ignorant and unstable twist to their own
> destruction, as they do the other scriptures.
>
> 2 Pet. 3.14-16, RSV

By the late first and early second century CE the letters of Paul were
widely appreciated in many parts of the church as a source of wisdom.
The fact that Paul had written his letters to churches about various
particular issues in congregational life provided for the possibility of
the reinterpretation and reapplication of what Paul had taught in one
generation to the life of the church in other contexts and in subsequent
generations. Nonetheless from this opportunity there also arose some
peril. In light of the fact that Paul had written to address specific
situations and contexts, how were churches to find timeless wisdom
and guidance for their different situations and contexts? The church
was faced with the dilemma: Paul's words bore the authority of his
wisdom and ministry, and yet it was not entirely clear what those
words meant for a new generation of various churches.

1 Timothy is a late first or early second-century text written in the
name of Paul which, much like the expressions in Polycarp's letter to
the Philippians and 2 Peter, grappled to re-engage the wisdom and
authority of Paul. In the name of Paul, the writer of 1 Timothy (as in
2 Timothy and Titus) sought to extend the wisdom, vision and reach of
Paul's authority and teaching to the church of his generation. As
Polycarp notes for the Philippians this is precisely what Paul would do
in his own ministry when he was away from his churches: he would
write them a letter. In this way the letter had become a viable
substitute for Paul's presence. And yet as a substitute it could not

represent Paul purely (much as his own letters could not), and in fact provided a representation, a projection and therefore a distortion of Paul.

This commentary on 1 Timothy engages the letter in two ways: as a response to the crisis of Paul's absence in the church, and as a necessary distortion of Paul into the theological and ecclesiological purposes of the actual writer of the letter. In this vein the commentary attempts both an empathetic interpretation of the letter, and a critical one as it tracks the ways in which the writer represents and projects Paul's teaching and vision for the church in particular ways. Seen in this way the interpretation of 1 Timothy provides an opportunity to watch the church at work within a particular historical context as it interpreted its traditions and attempted to discern their wisdom and authority in order to meet the changing situations and new crises of the church.

1 Timothy and the Pastoral Epistles

For its canonical life 1 Timothy has resided within a close ghetto of letters at the end of the Pauline corpus referred to as the 'Pastoral Epistles'. Only recently through Higher Critical investigation have the letters been designated together in a collection as 'the Pastorals', but earlier many church Fathers, and Protestant reformers alike noted their coherence in matters regarding church polity and doctrine. As such, 1 Timothy, 2 Timothy and Titus have been viewed as a group representing either the final personal communications from Paul to his most intimate acquaintances, or the pseudonymous reflections of a church leader to other church leaders charting the Pauline legacy according to his own course.

While modern scholars have largely assumed their unity and canonicity these three letters do have a somewhat complex and enigmatic history. In terms of ancient manuscript evidence for example, Vaticanus, the fourth-century codex of the Roman Catholic tradition, does not contain the three letters. Moreover, Jerome in his preface to a commentary on Titus, notes that Tatian (of the late second century CE) accepted Titus, but not 1 and 2 Timothy as authoritative (Duff, 582). Their arrangement in canon lists and codices that do contain them has varied. While some argue that the ultimate canonical arrangement of 1 Timothy, 2 Timothy and Titus is original (Dunn, 777), others have noted, following perhaps the Muratorian canon, which lists the letters 'and to Titus one, and to Timothy two', that Titus should precede 1 Timothy as an introduction to the collection, while 2 Timothy rounds out the set in testamentary form containing Paul's final wishes and testament (Quinn and Wacker, 8). All of these observations underscore the difficulty in classifying the letters as a corpus. While they share many of the same themes and vocabulary, both their reception and interpretation histories have challenged the notion that the letters speak with one voice and to the same single purpose.

In this light, it is a worthwhile endeavour to attend to the letters individually. Most modern commentators have taken them as a whole and have demonstrated cross-references and connections throughout (e.g. Bassler 1996), but this commentary will focus on one of the three, 1 Timothy. The text will be read primarily (with some exceptions) as a single unit. While the commentary will conceptualize 1 Timothy as a part of a larger collection, the whole letter will be engaged as a particular rhetorical construction with its own themes and emphases. Through such a reading I hope that the particularities of 1 Timothy will be better understood, which may in turn provide a basis for appreciating the whole collection in a new light.

In general this commentary on 1 Timothy is informed by approaches to biblical interpretation that are often classified as 'postmodern'. More of a general perspective than a particular field of study, 'postmodern' biblical interpretation takes both a critical and complementary stand in relation to 'modern' approaches to biblical texts that ground the text's meaning in understanding it as an expression of an author within a historical period. Far from denying the importance of history, postmodern biblical interpretation moves from a limiting of the meaning of the text in the mind of its author, and understands the text as having multiple potential meanings. Postmodern approaches to biblical interpretation, therefore, are suspicious of attempts to name and universalize a single meaning of a text. Such suspicions arise from a critique of modern assumptions of universal history, progress and meaning. In his work *The Postmodern Explained*, theorist Jean-François Lyotard identifies some characteristic elements of postmodern critiques of modernity in relation to the subject of architecture:

> Postmodern architecture finds itself condemned to undertake a series of minor modifications in a space inherited from modernity, condemned to abandon a global reconstruction of the space of human habitation. The perspective then opens onto a vast landscape, in a sense that there is no longer any horizon of universality, universalism, or general emancipation to greet the eye of the postmodern man. (Lyotard, 76)

Postmodern interpretations of biblical texts, in their resistance to universal claims to truth, take seriously the contextual nature of meaning. In this approach the interpreter is acknowledged as a participant in the 'production of meaning' from the text. Moreover, the text itself is understood as complex, and multivocal. Finally, the text's historical setting is understood not so much as a backdrop for the author's experience, as it is a politically charged context of competing political and social agendas.

Questions about the authorship of 1 Timothy

No contemporary critical discussion of 1 Timothy can avoid the issue of its authorship. For over a century the interpretation of the Pastoral Epistles (PE) in general has been embroiled within the controversy of their authenticity with regard to the Apostle Paul. From a postmodern perspective, one might argue that the critical method that has organized criteria out of the canonical letters about what is 'true' Paul and what is 'false' Paul is itself on shaky ground of becoming a 'universalizing' claim to the meaning of the letters. Construing the personality of a single author (in this case 'Paul') from a few letters, some of them fragmentary and corrupt in and of themselves, is a fabrication based upon modern commitments to reading texts as the pure expressions of their author's intentions. Despite the postmodern critique of such historical positivism, however, the conversation of critical scholarship about the entire Pauline corpus cannot be fully discounted. As these letters are ancient elements of communication, they are helpfully read with attention to matters regarding who may have written them, and to whom they may have been written. I understand this approach to represent a critical perspective on the contextual setting of the letters, be it modern or postmodern. The current reading of 1 Timothy will therefore consider the text as 'authored', and participate within scholarly conjecture (knowing it to be just that) regarding the letter's possible historical context and rhetorical purposes.

In addition to the letter's authorship, the identity of its receiver(s) is also an important element of its interpretation. Just as the authorship of Paul is understood by most scholars to be an element of pseudonymity in the letter's construction, so too the named recipient of the letter, 'Timothy', is also considered a pseudonym. In this, scholars have noted that it and the other PE are examples of 'double pseudonymous' writings (Bassler 1996). As such they contrive a particularly private space of communication between men who had become for the PE writer legendary founders of churches in Asia Minor. The promise of this contrivance in rhetorical terms is that their communication would bear the authority of a once lost but now found trove of instruction about 'how to behave in the household of God, the pillar and bulwark of truth' (1 Tim. 3.14). In the contentious time of the late first and early second-century interpretation of Paul among different churches such letters would represent the 'last word' on Paul's understanding of how the church should be in the world.

In the uncontested letters of Paul Timothy is often cited as a co-sender in the opening greetings (e.g. 2 Cor. 1.1, 1 Thes. 1.1, Phil. 1.1). As such he is remembered as one who wrote with Paul to churches. In addition, Paul describes Timothy in the uncontested letters as one who preaches with Paul and who is sent in Paul's stead to be with churches and to carry out Paul's ministry (e.g. Rom. 16.21, 1 Cor. 16.10, 2 Cor. 1.19, Phil. 2.19). Likewise Luke introduces Timothy in Acts 16.1-3 as a disciple (*mathetes*), the son of a Jewish woman believer and a Greek father, who has a good reputation in the churches of Lystra and Iconium and who Paul chooses to accompany him following his separation from Barnabas. The selection of Timothy as the recipient of 1 and 2 Timothy evokes the legacy of one whom Paul entrusted to 'stand in' for him as a preacher and a teacher of his churches, particularly in Asia Minor. It evokes the legacy of one whom Paul trusted entirely with his ministry. In this sense the use of Timothy's name as a recipient of Paul's teaching about how to behave in the church associates these letters with the reliable stewardship of Paul's words and ministry.

While the debate about authorship has consumed the study of the PE in just the last century, their checkered reception in the early church may mirror the current contentions about them. As noted above, the PE have a complex history of transmission in the early church. The most ancient papyrus containing evidence of a Pauline corpus, P 46, does not contain the writings. The list of Marcion's authoritative writings (dated to the early second century CE) does not contain or refer to the PE. The earliest stages of the canonization of the Christian Bible, therefore, are somewhat blurry on the existence, authority and placement of 1 Timothy, 2 Timothy and Titus.

In contrast to the spotty presence of 1 and 2 Timothy and Titus in the manuscript tradition of the New Testament canon, the literature of the early church Fathers contains many references to the letters. The early second-century Bishop of Smyrna, Polycarp seems to know of 1 Timothy, or at least several of the traditions cited within the letter in his Epistle to the Philippians. In his letter there appear to be two citations of the traditions in 1 Timothy 6.7–10: 'The love of money is the root of all evil', and 'as we brought nothing into this world, so we could bring nothing out' (*Pol.* 4). Later in the letter the bishop demands that deacons should not be 'double-tongued', echoing 1 Tim. 3.8 (*Pol.* 5). Still later he exhorts the Philippians to pray for kings, which reflects the call in 1 Timothy 2.2 (*Pol.* 12). In the third century CE, Tertullian in his refutations of Marcion's teachings indicates that he knows of 1 and 2 Timothy and Titus as he ponders why Marcion would accept Paul's personal letter to Philemon into his list of authoritative letters and yet not list the personal letters of 1 and 2 Timothy and Titus (*Against Marcion*, 5.21). It is clear that, while some elements of the early church did not know of the PE, other portions, notably those concerned with the promotion of orthodoxy, knew them well and cited them as authoritative.

Beyond the manuscript and transmission history, 1 Timothy and the other PE do represent a decidedly different language, church structure and context than the undisputed Pauline letters (Romans, 1 and 2 Corinthians, Galatians, Philippians, 1 Thessalonians and Philemon). Such internal evidence has also strengthened scholars' assertions regarding the pseudepigraphical nature of the PE. Not only is the vocabulary quite different from that of Paul's seven uncontested letters, but Paul's preoccupation with certain issues, such as the relationship of Jews to Gentiles, also seems to be missing. In the place of Paul's concerns are wholly new issues, such as opponents who appear to be ascetic and potentially Gnosticizing. Again, this seems to indicate a historical context quite a bit later than that of Paul. Moreover, church structure has a different cast in the PE. Where church offices do not appear to be fully established in Paul's correspondence, the PE assume distinct positions of bishop, deacon and potentially even 'widow'. These offices appear to be attached to policies regarding compensation, as well as expected protocols of behaviour (von Lipps). Generally speaking, while Paul's letters are charged with his personal urgency to maintain and restore relationships with his churches, the PE assume the existence and stability of the church. In this regard the PE seem to represent a decidedly different ecclesial and historical context to the uncontested letters of the Pauline corpus.

Another element of the distance between the letters and those of the historical Paul is that they resemble letters in outward form only. Many scholars have noted that in contrast to the occasional elements of Paul's letters such as 1 Thessalonians or 1 Corinthians, 1 Timothy and Titus are filled with orders for worship and church polity that resemble aspects of second-century ecclesiastical manuals such as the *Didache* and the *Apostolic Constitutions*. In his form critical commentary on the PE Martin Dibelius notes that in part 1 Timothy contains material that closely parallels the church orders of the *Didache* (e.g. *Did.* 7–10 and 1 Tim. 2.1; *Did.* 14 and 1 Tim. 2.8; and *Did.* 15.1, 2 and 1 Tim. 3.1), and in part 1 Timothy and Titus contain material that resembles a table of rules for the household, for example, the comportment of old men and women, the behaviour of church leaders, of widows and of slaves (Dibelius and Conzelmann, 6). In addition 1 Timothy and Titus, while drawn in the style of Paul's personal letters (such as Philemon), are not thoroughly engaged in personal communication. They present the outward form of the personal letter, but 1 Timothy lacks a thanksgiving and closes simply with 'grace be with you' and without Paul's customary greetings to others or references to his travel plans.

Such evidence has led many scholars to argue that the letters are not first-century writings of the Apostle Paul, but late first-century or early second-century documents written in his name. Seen in this light, the letters can be facilely dismissed as a set of frauds. Written falsely in Paul's name they steal his authority in order to define the church and its structure according to the theology and ecclesiology of the actual letter writer. The common terminology used to refer to the Pauline tradition underscores this assessment. Those letters written by the apostle are often called the 'authentic' letters of Paul in contrast to those that are pseudepigraphical in nature. As such, the study of Pauline theology and ecclesiology has in many ways focused on Romans, 1 and 2 Corinthians, Galatians, Philippians, 1 Thessalonians and Philemon, while the later letters of the canonical Pauline pseudepigraphical tradition (Ephesians, Colossians, 2 Thessalonians, 1 and 2 Timothy and Titus) have been less explored. In this commentary on 1 Timothy, Romans, 1 and 2 Corinthians, Galatians, Philippians, 1 Thessalonians and Philemon will be referred to as a group as the 'uncontested letters of Paul'. This designation notes that most scholars can agree that the historical Paul wrote at least these letters. With this label the letters are categorized not with reference to some idea of 'authentic' as opposed to 'fake', but rather with regard to the ongoing scholarly discussion about them.

In terms of attending to the thinking and situation of the historical Paul the division in study between the 'authentic' letters and the pseudepigraphical tradition is an understandable and important development. Through such a division scholars have appreciated the particularly apocalyptic and mystical aspects of the historical Paul's thought which is most vivid in the uncontested letters. In addition scholars have discerned the ascetic elements of Paul's ministry and its counter-cultural force. In terms of appreciating the church and its history, however, the later letters represent a fertile ground for exploration. Indeed as pseudepigraphical letters they are a part of the interpretation of Paul, and can be seen as one perspective in a late first-century and early second-century debate about the interpretation of the teachings of the Apostle Paul and the nature of the church. It is in just such a spirit that my examination takes up matters related to the authorship and intended audience of 1 Timothy. As such this commentary does not so much seek to prove the pseudepigraphical nature of the letter and thereby prove its 'inauthenticity'. Rather, this commentary assumes the pseudepigraphical nature of the letter and is interested in viewing 1 Timothy as a site for exploring a multivocal argument about Paul's theological legacy and the church both in ancient and contemporary settings. In this sense, the present commentary is interested in examining the text of 1 Timothy as a discourse.

Reading 1 Timothy as discourse - postmodern biblical interpretation

The notion of approaching a biblical text as a site of discourse is one that understands biblical interpretation to be about discerning dynamics of power. The Bible has long been studied in relation to power. The whole notion of the authority of scripture alive in Protestant biblical hermeneutics and renewed by contemporary Christian fundamentalisms is vitally concerned with issues of power. Such understandings, however, are generally concerned with how the text itself has the authority (or power) to direct the church or individual Christians in the life of Christian faith. Discourse analyses of biblical texts, on the other hand, examine the dynamics of power within the text and its various contexts of interpretation. Such approaches to the study of texts in general and Scripture in particular are focused on the social dimensions of the text both in its production and its interpretation throughout history. As such the modern approach to the historical context of the writing of the text is broadened from its focus on the 'author' of the text and his/her (usually his) intentions to a focus on the political dimensions of the text, which include the author and his possible intentions as well as the various other voices apparent within the text and its interpretive history. This shift in focus might generally be described as a development from a modern 'scientific' historical approach to the text to a postmodern 'ethical' consideration of the text's effects (both intended and unintended) in the various interpretive contexts of the text (not limited to its 'original' context). In her ground-breaking hermeneutical work Elisabeth Schüssler Fiorenza has variously described this approach as 'liberationist–cultural', 'rhetorical–political', 'pastoral–theological' and 'rhetorical–ethical'. Such an approach marks a pragmatic ground that seeks not simply to understand what a text meant historically, or how it is multivalent literarily, but how it is politically charged in its meaning in different interpretations, in different contexts. Such a process, according to Schüssler Fiorenza, is one of becoming conscious of and honest about the constructed nature of all knowledge and therefore the politically involved nature of all interpretation.

> Biblical interpretation is not just something for the intellectual 'ivory tower' or the clerical ghetto. Rather, biblical inquiry is important for all of us. In the open 'school house' of Wisdom we learn to ask: How has biblical interpretation been used and how is the bible still used either to protect powerful interests or to challenge them and engender socio-cultural, political, and religious change? How has the bible been used to define public discourse and groups of people? What are the mechanisms that obscure the cultural understanding of society and religion that is articulated in and through biblical texts? (Schüssler Fiorenza, 2001: 46)

The interpretation of 1 Timothy as a discourse is an approach that is concerned with the internal dynamics of power present within the text and its ancient historical context, as well as its external effects on contemporary church and culture. Viewing the text as a discourse is a means to ascertaining the voices within both the text and its interpretive history, including the voices of the author and editors, as well as the voices of those people in and around the PE writer's church that can be heard from between the lines of the text.

Reading between the lines

> Let a woman learn in silence and full submission. I permit no woman to teach or have authority over a man; she is to keep silent.
> 1 Tim. 2.11-12, NRSV

'You don't tell women to shut up, unless they are talking.' That comment made by a student with regard to the above text from 1 Timothy in a course I taught on women and scripture several years ago still rings in my ears. I think it still rings because it is true. More than that, it rings because it provided a crux in my articulation of a hermeneutical dilemma that I was facing regarding biblical texts like 1 Timothy 2.11-12. I was bothered by how I as a woman, and a student of these texts, who trains women and men for ordained Christian ministry in the interpretation of the Bible could claim a text like 1 Timothy 2.11-12 to have religious authority. This is a crisis that other feminist and liberationist interpreters have faced before me concerning much of the Bible. How do we claim texts that openly discredit our voices, our equality and our authority to be Holy Scripture, the inspired Word of God? Feminist interpreter Luise Schottroff summarizes the problem well in her work *Lydia's Impatient Sisters: A Feminist Social History of Early Christianity*:

> A new understanding of the canon is needed: it is a document of a history of contempt for human beings, of a history burdened with guilt. And yet at one and the same time it is the gospel. The life-giving gospel will surely not suffer damage when Christian women and men face up to the history of Christianity, tainted as it is with contempt for women, colonialism, persecution of Jews, and its traffic with patriarchy.
>
> (Schottroff, 78)

In my class the student's comment captured for me the notion that the text is not merely what it says. Of course I had known this at some level as I had affirmed a critical approach to the interpretation of scripture. Such an approach, to my mind, is one that examines the complexity of the text and its redaction and transmission history. In addition, it examines the context of the text historically, as well as the various contexts of its interpretation, including my context as an interpreter. It is a complex hermeneutical endeavour, in other words, to discern what a text 'meant' and what it 'means'. In this case, for me, the student's words cut concisely to the issue of voice. The text has a voice. Specifically 1 Timothy 2.8-15 has a voice that commands women to silence. Behind that seemingly singular voice, however, there are other voices. For example, there are the voices of women who are being commanded to silence, and perhaps other voices of those who actually listened to these women talk in the first place. I was reminded that the text, even though its author might like his audience to think so, is not monolithic.

Russian philosopher and literary theorist Mikhail Bakhtin described the multivocal nature of the text of the novel with the concept of 'heteroglossia'. For Bakhtin, language is filled with tension and that always has a political dimension. That political dimension is one of struggle in which claims to authenticity and ideological unity are always challenged (Vice, 20). Theologian and cultural theorist Wendy

Doniger has enjoined Bakhtin's theory of language in the novel to illumine the study of sacred texts and myths. Her insights provide a glimpse into how a text, as apparently monovocal and unanimous about the nature of the church as 1 Timothy, might be cracked open in order to hear the voices of those who have been marginalized and apparently 'silenced'.

> Bakhtin has taught us to recognize competing voices in the novel and different interpretive communities within the same text; we can, with profit, use Bakhtinian concepts of multivocality not only to bring women's voices into texts written by men but also to bring the voices of texts composed in one culture into texts composed in other cultures. (Doniger, 85)

Through the lenses of Bakhtin and Doniger, I have come to see that rather than a megaphone commanding silence, 1 Timothy 2.8-15 is a site in which there is an argument about who has a voice and why. All of a sudden the text has opened up for me in new ways. Where it had seemed to close doors, it now presents possibilities. Rather than an edict to silence women, 1 Timothy 2.8-15 has become transformed into a debate about who can and cannot have a voice in the church. Not only did this seem to be an incredibly relevant site for the exploration of contemporary Christian ministry, it also appeared to be something I could affirm as 'true'. The power to speak is indeed something women have fought about for a long time, from the very origins of the church. For its role, even unwitting, in preserving this argument I now affirm 1 Timothy 2.11-12 as 'Holy Scripture'.

The theoretical insights of Bahktin regarding the multivocality of texts are powerfully affirmed in the historical-critical researches of scholars into the nature of the theology of the early church and its writings. The work of F. C. Baur and Walter Bauer illumine the historical complexities behind a text such as 1 Timothy and open its interpretation from simply attending to its constructed claims of theology and church to attending to the crises and struggles through which such claims are being made. In the nineteenth century F. C. Baur noted that the portrait of the church and its history as told in Luke's Acts of the Apostles was motivated by dogmatic concerns for creating unity in a climate that was indeed tremendously diverse theologically and highly contentious ecclesiologically. To this insight he brought careful historical analysis of the tensions between what he overdrew as 'Petrine' and 'Pauline' aspects of the theological conflicts within the early church. A straightforward comparison of the discrepancies between Luke's portrayal of the Jerusalem Council in

Acts 15 and Paul's own description of his relationship with the Jerusalem church in Galatians 1–2 provides insight into the tensions that Baur sought to understand.

In the early twentieth century Walter Bauer brought nuance to Baur's observations with his landmark analysis of the multiple and diverse contexts of the development of the churches in the earliest centuries of Christianity. The work has been translated into English as *Orthodoxy and Heresy in Earliest Christianity*. Through the contextual sensitivity of his historical analyses Bauer argued the point that orthodoxy was not an original state from which developed later heresies. Rather ecclesial expressions later designated 'orthodox' by the centralizing powers of the church from the fourth century CE on, were in some cases later developments than those expressions deemed as 'heretical'. Thus, Bauer raised the rigorous historical insight that 'heresy' was not a departure from an original 'orthodox' Christianity. Interestingly in light of Bahktin's theory of multivocality in texts, Bauer's reflections on this complex appreciation of early Christian theologies engage the metaphor of voice:

> if we follow such a procedure and simply agree with the judgment of the anti-heretical fathers of the post-New Testament period, do we not all too quickly become dependent upon the vote of but one party – that party which perhaps as much through favorable circumstances as by its own merit eventually was thrust into the foreground, and which possibly has at its disposal today the more powerful, and thus, more prevalent voice, only because the chorus of others has been muted? (Bauer, xxi)

According to Bauer's analyses, Christian communities were incredibly diverse with regard to practice, belief and, notable for this commentary, the interpretation of Paul's writings during the late first and early second century. Bauer's insights reveal that there is more to the claims of the texts of early Christianity than what one might first hear. Attending to the multiple perspectives voiced within Christian writings is a means to discerning the texts not simply as the authors' perspectives, but as sites of competing power relations. In the case of 1 Timothy, the letter writer interprets Paul's teaching and legacy in ways that engage with the interpretation of Paul in other Christian communities. In such a perspective the text of 1 Timothy is not simply a relic of the church's history or a dogmatic claim of the church's organization, but an expression of desire about the nature of the church and its life in the world. As such an expression it can be critiqued, challenged, and perhaps agreed with, but it can never stand on its own as a singular statement of the truth. In this sense the authority (or power) of a text such as 1 Timothy is not denied, but it is mediated differently than in more traditional ecclesial exegetical practice.

The historical insights of Baur and Bauer and those who have followed their interpretations of the diversity of the early church have laid an important foundation for the feminist and liberationist researches of scholars such as Elisabeth Schüssler Fiorenza and Luise Schottroff. This is so in that the historical sensitivity to the contentious and multiple expressions of the early Christian writings goes far toward troubling the monolithic authority of the PE writer's and other NT texts' claims about women's roles in the church. In her assessment of the PE tradition, for instance, Schüssler Fiorenza argues for the 'prescriptive' as opposed to the 'descriptive' nature of the PE writer's rhetoric. In this sense, the PE do not describe the 'reality' of the church as it followed after Paul, but rather seek to prescribe a way of being church in the midst of what was for the PE writer a troubling diversity of expressions of theology, ecclesiology and ethics.

> Patriarchalization of the early Christian movement and ascendancy of the monarchical episcopacy not only made marginal or excluded women leaders in the early church but also segregated and restricted them to women's spheres, which gradually came under the control of the bishop. Nevertheless, it must be emphasized again that the writings suggesting this kind of patriarchal dynamic are prescriptive rather than descriptive, since the male clergy were often dependent upon wealthy and influential women even into late antiquity. Ideological prescription and actual social reality do not always correspond. (Schüssler Fiorenza 1984: 310)

Likewise Luise Schottroff has noted the political rhetorical purposes of the PE writer at work in 1 Timothy. Schottroff argues that 1 Timothy is an example of misogynistic discourse with many parallels in Greco-Roman literature. She observes, contrary to much contemporary apologetic interpretation of the text, that the letter serves to proscribe certain activities for women not merely in worship, but also in everyday life. In spite of this agenda, however, Shottroff claims that the letter 'also documents women's liberation struggles in an unwitting, but interesting manner' (Schottroff, 73). She discerns, much as my student did, that between the lines of 1 Timothy there is an alternative history of women's resistance to their oppression, and a testimony to their struggle for liberation in the early church: 'First Timothy was to bring an end to this history of women's liberation, to discredit and render it invisible' (Schottroff, 73). This current interpretation of 1 Timothy intends to read between the lines to chart the resistance movements evident in the letter's discourse. It will attend to the issues of power evident within the voice of the letter writer, and the voices of those whom he seeks to sideline and silence. In this sense, the letter provides an opportunity in the legacies of F. C. Baur and Walter Bauer to read the history of the church as a history not so much of one-sided domination, but of ongoing struggle.

Hebrew Bible scholars Dana Nolan Fewell and David Gunn in their work *Gender, Power, and Promise: The Subject of the Bible's First Story* claim the richness and multivocality of texts in relation to the narratives of Genesis through 2 Kings. Their practice is to read against the grain of the text in order to produce readings that take seriously the experience of women within the stories, and resist the drive to gloss over elements of the narrative that do not conform to predetermined theological convictions. In the introduction to their book they discuss their method of interpretation and note that most interpretations of biblical texts work hard at making the entire text cohere and portray a single voice. Their method is to undo this project, to challenge the constructed coherence of the text.

> Consequently we have learned to be more suspicious readers, with an eye for the subliminal construction of the norm and the different. ... We have learned to seek out the different and the discordant, the puzzling element in the text that is usually bypassed or harmonized, and to build a reading around it. That is like seeking out loose threads in a sweater and by pulling them carefully observing the garment's (de)construction. No persuading voice can make its case without acknowledging, even if only implicitly, the voices that speak against it (Fewell and Gunn, 16)

In 1 Timothy, 2 Timothy and Titus, the constructed voice of the Pastoral Epistle writer is attempting to be very persuasive with his church. While Fewell and Gunn are interpreting narratives of the Hebrew Bible in their work, this current commentary picks up their approach in the interpretation of an early Christian epistle.

In 1 Timothy the voice of the letter writer appears to be immediately available. At times he speaks in the first person, and at other times he issues second-person imperatives and hortatory subjunctives in order to address his audience. The letter writer's voice speaks with a great deal of authority. That authority, however, is both deepened and complicated by the letter writer's assumption of the identity and voice of the Apostle Paul. As, following Fewell and Gunn, we hear the letter writer's voice not as the 'natural' voice of Paul, but as a manufactured voice that is vested with rhetorical purpose, we begin to pull at the threads of the letter's construction. Doing so begins to deconstruct the persuasive voice of the letter writer and to reveal his anxieties, ambiguities, contradictions and even the implicit voices of those whom he seeks to silence and supervise.

Reading a text in order to challenge its coherence and to reveal its construction is a necessarily antagonistic endeavour. As Fewell and Gunn note above, their approach is suspicious. Many feminist interpreters have taken what has been termed a 'hermeneutic of suspicion' toward both the texts of the Bible and their history of interpretation in order to challenge scripture's androcentric and patriarchal nature. Such a posture does not take the text at face value, but mines the text and its various contexts for the voices and perspectives of those who have been pushed to the margin. The text of 1 Timothy in this approach provides a space in which to wrestle with the letter writer and his various claims about the church and the nature of the Christian community. In such an antagonistic posture there are voices to be heard in between the lines.

As I have read further into the letter it has become clear to me that the writer of 1 Timothy was attempting to assert his voice in a larger argument that has raged in the church in the centuries following Paul (and in many ways still rages today). Attending to his voice while at the same time trying to discern the elements of power in the text is a delicate balance. One must be empathetic enough with the writer to engage his concerns and appreciate his predicament, yet at the same time understand that there are others around him who would disagree with the way in which he envisions the church, and whose voices and perspectives need attention as well. Indeed his is a single voice within the larger war of words.

A voice in a war of words

Contemporary critical scholarship on 1 Timothy, as well as 2 Timothy and Titus, has focused on many of the letters' referents to heretical teachings and opponents in the church. These studies have hypothesized that the letter writer refutes expressions of Christianity that were emerging in the second century, e.g. Gnosticism, Marcionism and forms of mystical Judaism. While there are some grounds for these hypotheses, the scholarly quest to reconstruct the letter writer's opponents has led to a lack of attention to the rhetoric he uses to refute them and how that rhetoric may inform interpreters of his location. Indeed, the letter writer's use of the genre of pseudepigraphy has been seen not so much as a rhetorical tool (with the important exception of the excellent study by Lewis Donelson (1986)), as a necessary extension of the Apostle's authority to refute heretics.

The necessary refutation of heresy requires an assumption of an established orthodoxy. Critical study of the church in the second century demonstrates that no such assumption can be made for that time (e.g. Bauer, Koester). What becomes clear through an examination of the interpretation of Paul in canonical and non-canonical second-century literature is that Marcion and Marcionites (Harnack 1901), the Gnostics (Pagels 1979), the *Acts of Paul* communities (MacDonald 1983) as well as the 'orthodox' communities all fervently interpreted Paul's letters. In this light the use of pseudepigraphy by the PE writer is not so much a necessary extension of Paul, as it is a rather innovative power play in the midst of a contentious climate around the interpretation of the Apostle and the organization of the church.

In the historical effort of reconstructing opponents, another thing commentators have tended to overlook is the extent to which the letter writer's rhetoric is obsessed with the issue of language. When the letter writer addresses those who do wrong it is their speech that is critiqued. It is vain discussion (*mataiologian*, 1.6), blaspheming (1.20), speaking out of both sides of the mouth (*dilogous*, 3.8), gossiping (*phluaroi*, 5.13), 'saying what one should not' (5.13), being controversial and disputing about words (6.4) that cause the letter writer the most concern. With these ills the letter writer contrasts the sureness of sayings (*pistos o logos*, 1.15, 3.1a), the soundness of the words of Jesus Christ (6.3), the good confession (*ten kalen homologian*, 6.12), and the project of keeping the commandment unstained (6.14). The correct words for the letter writer seem to have the ultimate significance of salvation or damnation. Timothy himself is instructed: 'Take heed to yourself and to your teaching, hold to that, for by doing so you will save both yourself and your hearers' (4.16).

In the light of the letter writer's concern with language, the use of the convention of pseudepigraphy can be seen anew. The letter writer, through his use of Paul's name, is not merely trying to extend the Apostle's authority into a new generation. Rather, the letter writer is claiming Paul's voice and Pauline language in the midst of a climate that is in conflict about how to interpret Paul's letters, how to interpret the language of the emerging tradition. Concern for legitimate as opposed to illegitimate speech can be seen alongside legitimate and illegitimate interpretation of Paul and his teachings regarding the church. In a situation where Marcion, Gnostics, Pneumatics, Montanists and others all claimed Paul's writings as authoritative, the PE letter writer goes to the source, and speaks his interpretation of

Paul by appropriating the voice of the Apostle himself. In this sense he fortifies his words with the direct and unfettered authority of Paul.

As was noted from the work of Fewell and Gunn above, 'no persuading voice can make its case without acknowledging, even if only implicitly, the voices that speak against it' (Fewell and Gunn, 16). This reading of 1 Timothy is interested not only in attending to the voice of the letter writer and the voices of those around him, but also to the way the letter writer's construction of the authoritative voice of Paul contains expressions of his own inherent uncertainties and insecurities. As he speaks within the voice of Paul and constructs the space of intimate communication between Paul and Timothy, the letter writer seeks to construct a space of authority and clarity within the Pauline tradition. This space, however, is far from certain in his social and ecclesial reality. In this, the letter's language belies many tensions, ironies and ambiguities within the church and its traditions, particularly with regard to the desire for Christian unity and solidity. It is the hope of this current interpretation of 1 Timothy that such an investigation into the constructed nature of the letter writer's rhetoric will challenge the constructed certainties behind our own contemporary assumptions of 'church', 'tradition', what is considered 'orthodox' and what is deemed 'heretical'. In this sense, the investigation of 1 Timothy becomes an opportunity for reading contemporary Christian rhetorical expressions and decoding their constructed authorities and implicit persuasive purposes. Such a practice of interpretation becomes a way of attuning our sensitivities to issues of power and to its social-institutional effects in both ancient and contemporary practices of being 'church'.

The PE and the *Acts of Paul and Thecla*

Nowhere is it more apparent that the PE writer is engaged in a battle of words than when the claims of his three letters are laid alongside the traditions about Paul's itinerant ministry with a young woman of Ephesus named Thecla. The repository of these traditions is the apocryphal third-century text within the *Acts of Paul*, *The Acts of Paul and Thecla*. While the traditions were deemed 'forged' by the hands of a well-meaning, but (according to Tertullian) misguided Presbyter of Asia, many legendary figures of church history through the sixth century CE referred to the martyrdom of Thecla and her exemplary chastity: e.g. Cyprian, Eusebius, Augustine and Chrysostom. As such the tensions between the rhetoric of the *Acts of Paul and Thecla* and the PE regarding speech and particularly women's speech portray the broad parameters of the way in which the interpretation and representation of Paul and his teaching were employed in the debates about ecclesiology, social organization and mission in the early church.

The *Acts of Paul and Thecla* portrays the ministry of Paul as itinerant and committed to the preaching of the chaste and godly life. The tradition opens with a reference to Paul's preaching in Iconium. There he states a list of 'beatitudes', five of which uphold the blessing of those who are virgins, who have wives as though they have them not and who keep their flesh undefiled. This tradition seems informed directly by the teachings of Paul regarding virginity in 1 Corinthians 7. In response to this preaching in the legend Paul attracts the attention of a young, betrothed maiden, Thecla. Thecla becomes a devout listener to Paul's preaching and seeks to leave her home and obligation of betrothal and marriage to follow him in his ministry. As the drama plays out in Iconium, Thecla's mother, Theocleia, and Thecla's betrothed, Thamyris, seek to retain her within the system of the patriarchal household. As they react to Paul's teaching their rhetoric very much echoes that of the PE writer. In each case of their response to the problem they focus on the power of Paul's speech to pervert the minds of their women and upset the foundations of their social order. In response to the query of Thamyris about Paul's teaching, two characters known as Demas and Hermogenes respond: 'Who this man is we do not know. But he deprives young men of wives and virgins of husbands, saying, "Otherwise there is no resurrection for you, unless you remain chaste and do not defile the flesh but keep it pure."' Finally when Thamyris succeeds in compelling the crowd to drive Paul before the governor Castillus the crowd shouts at Paul: 'Away with the magician, because he has corrupted our women.'

In contrast to the Iconians' deep desire to cling to the social status quo in the face of Paul's transgressive speech, Paul himself is portrayed in the *Acts of Paul and Thecla* as one who does not assume or seek to defend the social structures of the patriarchal household. When in Antioch with Thecla Paul does not pretend to have a traditional relationship with her for either propriety's sake or for the sake of her safety. Indeed when a certain official named Alexander's queries Paul about his travel with Thecla he responds: 'She does not belong to me.' Given this window of opportunity, Alexander seizes Thecla on the street and kisses her. Thecla is forced to defend her chastity on her own (which she does quite well), as Paul stands idly by. Finally, after Thecla has devoted herself completely to following Paul he commissions her on her way back to Iconium: 'Go and teach the word of God.'

The Paul of the PE and the Paul of the *Acts of Paul and Thecla* stand in direct contrast to one another in their speech about women. The Paul of the PE demands 'I permit no woman to teach or have authority over a man' (1 Timothy 2.12) and the Paul of the *Acts of Paul* calls Thecla to 'go and teach the word of God'. This contrast shows how the authority and legend of Paul grew into two different traditions to support two radically different visions of church and social reality. Read in relationship with one another the two documents bespeak the struggle to claim Paul's authority by the radically different interpretations of his theology and vision of the church that had emerged in the late first and early second century. Throughout this commentary, at appropriate points in the interpretation of 1 Timothy the contrasting speech of the Paul of the *Acts of Paul and Thecla* will be cited and examined in order to hear examples of the 'implicit' voices that reside within the PE writer's directions about women and concerns regarding their behaviour. A critical edition of the text in English translation may be found in W. Schneemelcher's *The New Testament Apocrypha* (1991–92). English translations are widely available on the internet, notably the translation of M. R. James (1924) found at www.early-christianwritings.com and www.ccel.org. This commentary on 1 Timothy is very much informed by a reading of the *Acts of Paul and Thecla*. When a copy of the legend is set alongside the letter two sides of an ancient struggle within the church come into view, and the purposes of this commentary to read 1 Timothy for its multiple voices is well served.

The context of the war of words – the church of the late first and early second century in Asia Minor

In 1 Timothy 1.3 'Paul' reminds 'Timothy' of his command that Timothy remain in Ephesus while he moved on to Macedonia. Such references may or may not indicate the place of the letter's compostion. Given that 1 Timothy is a work of ancient pseudepigraphical epistolary correspondence, the details of its addresser, addressee and location must be understood as potential elements of the writer's deception. Proper names and place names are often added in this genre as a means of attaining verisimilitude. In handling the legend of Paul, no doubt, the city of Ephesus would offer an excellent place to locate Paul and Timothy's final correspondence. Before Paul headed westward to Rome Ephesus had been his base of operation.

Although the place name Ephesus may be a fiction, it also bears the possibility of being the letter writer's intended context for the letter's instructions. If the letter's recipients were to 'overhear' this private correspondence to Timothy at Ephesus when they themselves struggled to lead churches in Ephesus, the instructions allegedly intended for Timothy would have the powerful effect of directly addressing their experience. Walter Bauer notes that in their address to Ephesus 1 and 2 Timothy take up the orthodox ecclesial battle for the churches Paul had founded in that city (Bauer, 84–85). Indeed Paul's own letters make reference to the trouble of adversaries in Ephesus who oppose his teaching (e.g. 1 Cor. 15.32, 1 Cor. 16.8-9). In addition, much in concert with 1 and 2 Timothy, Luke in Acts 20.30 portrays Paul predicting to the elders (*presbuteroi*) at Ephesus: 'Some even from your own group *will come* distorting the truth in order to entice the disciples to follow them' (NRSV, emphasis mine). In the late first century Ephesus was an area of diverse Christian belief and practice. It became a battleground that Christians of the emerging orthodoxy (such as Luke and the PE writer) portrayed Paul himself decades earlier struggling to hold. The PE writer's choice to address 'Timothy' in the city of Ephesus could simply seek to recreate the historical verisimilitude of a correspondence between Paul and his follower, but it could also represent the writer's attempt to gain control over the leadership of the church in that particular city.

The region of Asia Minor, of which Ephesus is a western coastal city, is portrayed in early Christian writings as a hotbed of division regarding practice and belief. Paul himself in his letter to the churches in Galatia reserves some of his most heated rhetoric for his opponents in Asia Minor (e.g. Gal. 5.12). John the Seer in Revelation 1.4–3.22 presents his seven letters to seven churches in Asia that describe the struggle of competing prophets and teachers in the cities of Pergamum (Rev. 2.14-15) and Thyatira (Rev. 2.2-24). In the letter to Ephesus John relates that the church has successfully tested their false prophets (Rev. 2.2), but, as Bauer notes, the theologies of John the Seer and the PE writer do not conform to one another. John and the PE writer, for example, would never agree about the relation of the church to the Roman Empire. In this regard John's sanguine assessment of the Ephesian church may not have met with the PE writer's agreement, revealing further diversity in the church there. Finally, the *Acts of Paul and Thecla*, reviewed earlier, represents a provenance of Asia Minor, with Thecla's hometown of Iconium, and travel to Antioch. In light of John the Seer's conflict with the prophetess in Thyatira whom he describes as 'teaching and beguiling my servants to practise fornication and eat food sacrificed to idols' (*Jezebel*, Rev. 2.20-24), one wonders if a dispute over the interpretation of Paul's teaching about food sacrificed to idols in 1 Corinthians 8-10 may be in view. Whatever the exact content of these disagreements, it is clear that the Christianity of Asia Minor in the late first and early second century CE was generally diverse, and particularly divided in its interpretation of Paul's teaching. As a letter written to Ephesus, 1 Timothy occupies the space of one perspective within the church's diverse and contentious debate about the legacy of Paul.

Re-imagining the relationship of 1 Timothy to the Pauline tradition

Viewing 1 Timothy as a voice in a larger war about words is a means of reclaiming its interpretation. For the most part critical interpretation of the PE has seen them in either of two lights in relationship to the seven 'authentic' letters of Paul. In some circles, the PE have been viewed as the 'maturing' of the Pauline tradition into the 'real world'. Such interpretations understand that the imminent sense of eschatology and the social structures of a community living in that expectation could not be long sustained. Indeed, between Paul's earlier writings (such as 1 Thessalonians) and his later writings (such as Romans), these scholars detect a relaxing of imminent eschatological expectation. In this perspective 1 and 2 Timothy and Titus represent a point along a trajectory of cultural accommodation and institutional development already begun in Paul. If this view of accommodation is accepted then the letters' claims about roles within the community, and view of disputes are in continuity with Paul's ministry. They represent the necessary trajectory that developed out of Paul in order that the church might be sustained as an established institution in the midst of second-century pressures of heresy and cultural forces.

In his commentary on 1 Timothy, 2 Timothy and Titus Raymond Collins represents this assessment of the necessary accommodation of Paul's theology in the challenging context of the late first-century world. In an apology for the PE writer's treatment of women in 1 Timothy 2.8-15 he states:

> The Pastor's Midrash on the creation narrative (1 Timothy 2.13-15) is to be understood within the context of this search for an appropriate use of the Jewish Scriptures by the community. As does Paul (1 Cor. 6.16) and the Synoptics (Matt. 19.4-6; Mark 10.6-8), the Pastor uses the Genesis creation narratives as the basis on which the male-female relationship is to be understood. In the Judaism of his day, only men were considered capable of teaching. . . . The Pastor's Halachah on

women (1 Tim. 2.13-15) is an appropriation of the Jewish tradition to
his own community.

That appropriation occurred within the Hellenistic culture of the
Greco-Roman world in which the Pastor and his community lived.
Jewish Christian communities living closer to the time of Jesus than
did the Hellenistic Christian communities of the late first century
were able to profit from the tolerance accorded to Jews because of
the *religio licita* principle of Roman jurisprudence. A generation or
two later, when the expectation of an imminent Parousia had waned,
Hellenistic Christian communities had to find their own place in the
Greco-Roman world. (Collins, 74)

In contrast to the accommodationist approach outlined above, a more
negative critical assessment of the PE in their modern interpretation
understands the letters as representative of a 'fallen' Pauline
Christianity. Here the radical dissimilarity between the seven uncontested letters of Paul and the PE is emphasized. Such interpreters
understand that Paul envisioned a church of equals among men,
women, slaves, free, Jew and Gentile (Gal. 3.28), but the PE
demonstrate the establishment and justification of divisions in the
church on gender and class lines. Assessments of this development
credit the PE with establishing a bourgeois, culturally accommodated
church. 1 Timothy, 2 Timothy and Titus reflect a 'sell-out' of early
Christian values and ethics. Biblical critic James Barr presents a cogent
summary of this perspective on the PE and other 'late' texts within the
canon:

Thus the earlier text is not, because it is earlier, automatically
superior to the later, but the later, just because it is final, is certainly
not superior to the earlier. On the contrary, if we take the main
central material as our basis, in either Old or New Testament, it is
difficult to doubt that the approach to completeness is signalized by a
certain deterioration, by a failure to understand what the basic
insights of the contents of the traditions were, by a tendency to
compromise on the one hand and to harden into rigid systems on the
other. This can sometimes be seen in the latest touches added to
books, sometimes in the more marginal books added last to the
canon. Who will suppose, for instance, that 2 Peter really understood
Christianity as well as 1 Peter, or that letters to Timothy are in
theological content comparable with Romans or Galatians? (Barr, 93)

In both perspectives detailed above, 1 Timothy and the PE are viewed
as a single line out of Paul. They are understood either to sustain and
continue his legacy, or to betray it. Attending to the letter not as a
single development out of Paul, but rather as a voice in a debate about
him and the structure of the church changes its interpretation

tremendously. As a voice in a war of words about words 1 Timothy and the other letters of the PE corpus represent a part of an argument in early Christianity about the nature of the church. In their obsession with 'right speech' they mark a turn from the personality of the Apostle (in an ironic use of his personality, as pseudepigrapha) toward a focus on the tradition about him. As such, the PE seem to mark the creation of what they seek to defend. It is in this sense that their production and attachment to the other letters of Paul in the canon served as an extremely innovative rendering of Paul and the church in his name. Reading 1 Timothy as a part of this innovative moment is a way to appreciate the importance of these letters, as well as to locate their rhetoric not as necessary or naturally evolutionary, but as one claim about Paul's vision for the church in a larger array of claims. I hold that such an appreciation of their rhetoric provides an analogous way to think of our practice of Christian rhetoric today. An examination of the letter's content and structure reveals the rich connections the writing can provide for the study of ancient and contemporary Christianities.

The content and structure of 1 Timothy

The text of 1 Timothy is a complex weave of a variety of traditional forms combined with the letter writer's rhetorical connections and polemic. There are vice lists, household codes and various liturgical pieces (e.g. creeds, doxologies, prayers and hymns) peppered throughout the epistle. Moreover, the arrangement of these pieces is not always logical or clear. For example, the introduction of the letter is interpolated with a series of warnings against 'other teachings', and then resumes to a typical thanksgiving form (1 Tim. 1.3-11 and 1.12-17). Internally, however, there are logical links between items. For example, orders for the behaviour and qualifications of deacons follow immediately after those given for bishops (1 Tim. 3.1-13). In this sense, the letter appears to contain a variety of existing forms that have been edited together. In fact, the volume of traditional material has led some scholars to argue that 1 Timothy (as well as 2 Timothy and Titus) is a composite document made up of letter fragments, rather than a genuine letter in its own right (Miller, 18). Such insights about the heavy use of traditional material in the letters, and their loose literary structure certainly challenge the notion of a single author at work (be it Paul or a pseudepigrapher). Rather than speaking with a single voice, the letter bears voices of the early church in its practices of prayer, confession, polemic and praise. As much as it may hope to present a single vision for the church with all of its statements of certainty and unity (e.g. 1 Tim. 3.15: 'the church of the living God, the pillar and bulwark of the truth', NRSV), its diverse contents chafe within the constraints of such assertions. Moreover the letter writer's own polemic against his opponents reveals a complex picture of the early church with a variety of practices and beliefs.

The variety of traditional materials and the loose literary structure of 1 Timothy defy a facile description of the letter's unity or coherence. In addition to the variety of traditions and forms, the pseudepigraphical details that hold up the ruse of Paul's travel schedule, his biography, greetings and closing remarks are found throughout the writing. As noted earlier the letter says many things, including those things that it apparently argues against or attempts to silence. In this commentary each unit will be explored along the lines of discourse, and the whole will be appreciated for its multivocality.

1 Timothy in contemporary ecclesiological discourse

The structure of 1 Timothy reveals the writing to be a cache of particular ancient Christian practices and polemic. Such particularity would seem to limit the letter's importance in the general practice of the church. Such, however, could not be farther from the truth. The letter's interpretation throughout the church's history reveals that rather than a canonical afterthought, the claims of 1 Timothy have served as a fulcrum and justification for much of the practice and polity of contemporary Christianity. The words of 1 Timothy continue to provide the ammunition by which battles about the nature of the church and its human social organization are continuing to be waged.

Women and ministry

The above-cited text (1 Timothy 2.8-15) that mandates women to silence and prohibits their authority over men in the church has served and still serves today to justify the church's exclusion of women from leadership roles that bear authority over men. This has had far-reaching effects both within the church and broader culture. In the late nineteenth century the struggle of women for suffrage in the United States and Britain tangled directly with the church's application of the commands for women's silence and submission in 1 Timothy 2.8-15 (Stanton *et al.*, 161-68). More recently, the 14 June 2000 declaration of the Southern Baptist Convention in the US, *The Baptist Faith and Message* Section VI on 'Church', states that 'while both men and women are gifted for service in the church, the office of pastor is limited to men as qualified by Scripture'. The text cited for this claim is none other than 1 Timothy 2.9-14. Indeed current Roman Catholic doctrine also cites the text as part of the justification for the prohibition against women's ordination in the church.

The power of the claims of 1 Timothy 2.8-15 in the life of the church and surrounding cultures cannot be denied. The reach of these sentences through time and space, across the history of the church cannot be overestimated. The impact of these claims on the lives of women, not only with regard to their service in the church, but also in regard to their work in the domestic realm is enormous. Rather than an antiquated opinion of some late first or early second-century church father, these lines through their canonical location and attribution to Paul have lived and been circulated to circumscribe women's work and power with implications that reach today.

One particular example of the reach of 1 Timothy 2.8-15 can be seen in the tragedy of Andrea Yates, a Texas mother of five who drowned each of her own children in a bathtub. Ms Yates suffered terribly with mental illness and in particular with severe bouts of postpartum depression. Into the mix of this mental instability, Ms Yates was heavily involved in an evangelical conservative expression of Christianity where she and her husband came under the influence of the evangelist, Michael Peter Woroniecki. Reverend Woroniecki has published in his religious pamphlets and his newsletter entitled *Perilous Times* (named for the phrase found in 2 Tim. 3.1, KJV) that the biblical character Eve was a witch whose sin demanded atonement in the form of perfect motherhood (Pollitt, 10). No doubt the connection of Eve and atonement through childbearing was at least in part introduced to Woroniecki through the argument of the PE writer in 1 Timothy 2.13-15: 'For Adam was formed first, then Eve, and Adam was not deceived, but the woman being deceived was in the transgression. Notwithstanding she will be saved through childbearing, if they continue in faith and charity with holiness and sobriety' (KJV). Under this kind of pressure Andrea Yates could take her mental illness as a sign of her defectiveness as a mother. Again and again she told authorities after her arrest that she was freeing her children, having mercy on them by setting them free from such a terrible mother. For Yates, the combination of a particularly caustic interpretation of 1 Timothy 2.8-15 and mistreated mental illness resulted in a tragedy of epic proportion. The violence done through this text and its interpretation to this woman and through her to her family defies the notion that 1 Timothy and the other PE are simply ancient relics that can gather dust on the back shelf of the church's life. They are very much alive and require the constant reinvestigation and challenge of critical scholarship in each time and place.

Justifications for slavery

The text of 1 Timothy 6.1, 'Let all who are under the yoke of slavery regard their masters as worthy of all honor' (NRSV), was a widely cited text in the defences of slavery debates with abolitionists in the nineteenth century in the United States. While such use of biblical justification for human subjugation may be relegated to old historical squabbles from which we might imagine we have 'evolved', the text has been recently cited in a late twentieth-century political battle within the state of Alabama regarding the presence of the Confederate flag over the state capital. In this debate a particular state senator named Charles Davidson defended the use of the Confederate flag as an icon of Southern heritage, and defended the institution of slavery as legitimate because of its biblical warrant. In his argument he quoted both Leviticus 18 and 1 Timothy 6.1. Here he stated in his speech that the African slaves of the south were the best treated of any slaves in the history of humanity and that if someone wished to discredit slavery, they would be discrediting the Bible (Rawls 1996). Importantly, Davidson's remarks produced a large outcry across the United States, and he withdrew from the national congressional race shortly afterwards. Nonetheless, his speech demonstrates how a text such as 1 Timothy 6.1-2 can continue to have rhetorical force and life long past its original historical period and outside its original context. Furthermore, such a contemporary engagement of the text in political life provides further warrant for ongoing critical investigation of the text in its historical context and various contexts of interpretation and application.

Human sexuality

The text of 1 Timothy 1.10 is among a handful of biblical texts that are engaged in contemporary debates about human sexuality and the church (e.g. Lev. 18.22 and 20.13, Rom. 1.26–27, 1 Cor. 6.9). In particular these texts have been used to argue the biblical mandate that homosexuality is a sin. The Timothy citation appears to be a representation of the vice list cited in Paul's 1 Corinthians 6.9. Both are lists and both contain the term *arsenokoitas* that is translated in the NRSV as 'fornicator'. Despite its apparent role as a duplicate of

1 Corinthians 6.9, 1 Timothy 1.10 is often cited as further evidence that 'the Bible' is against homosexuality. For this reason Robert Goss, a scholar of religion and an advocate for the rights of homosexuals in church and society, has labelled this text a 'text of terror' (Goss, 90–91). It has been used historically to discredit the full participation of gay, lesbian, bisexual and transgendered persons in the life of the church. For its role in this stockpile of homophobic weaponry, the text of 1 Timothy 1.10 requires reinvestigation and critical engagement.

Conclusion

Just as the above-noted areas of social experiences connect 1 Timothy to contemporary ecclesial and cultural debates, less 'hot-button' issues also reveal a deep connection between the claims of 1 Timothy about the church and the life of the church today. For example many Christian churches reflect in their polity structures an ordering of church office between bishops, elders and deacons, or pastors, elders and deacons that connects with the polity expressions of 1 Timothy. As much as many Protestants might resonate with the theological tenacity and individuality of Paul in his seven uncontested letters, contemporary churches more realistically reflect the structures and practices of 1 Timothy and the other Pastoral Epistles. Clergy are generally financially compensated for their work, and there are regulations or guidelines in many denominational structures concerning the amount of compensation, and the nature of other benefits, including health insurance and pension plans. In this sense, 1 Timothy and the other Pastoral Epistles share more in common with contemporary churches than many might choose to recognize.

In addition to financial concerns, the expectations of doctrinal unity, and the emphasis on sound teaching that characterizes 1 Timothy, preoccupies much of contemporary ecclesial discourse. In this sense, the 'church' which the writer of 1 Timothy envisioned seems to have won the day historically speaking. Today most Christians cannot imagine church without ecclesiastical discipline, without orders of offices, without expectations of credal fidelity, and each of these components reflect the majority of the contents of 1 Timothy, 2 Timothy and Titus.

The PE in general, and 1 Timothy in particular may well seem stodgy and out of date in their particular expressions regarding women, human sexuality and human social organization; however, close attention to their rhetoric will reveal that most churches today have taken up their structure and practices, if not each and every one of their beliefs. For this reason, a critical return to the rhetoric of 1 Timothy is not so much simply a curiosity or a careful examination of an antique, but rather it is the work of assessing and attending to an expression of the church's business that is importantly connected to the life of the church today. It is a way of looking backward both to understand what the church was, and to understand more about what the church is in its various contemporary expressions.

1 Timothy 1.1-20:
Establishing the Pauline Legacy and
Addressing the Context

Introduction

As a whole 1 Timothy 1.1-20 provides a means by which the letter writer constructs the ruse of the intimate communication between Paul and Timothy. Throughout the chapter, as opposed to other sections of the letter, the writer continually refers to himself in the first person and refers directly to Timothy. As is common within Paul's epistles, the opening of the letter contains a greeting and reference to travel. This establishes the occasion for the letter. Paul has travelled from Ephesus, his base of operation for the Mediterranean mission, and has urged Timothy to remain in Ephesus to provide clear instructions and controls on the teachings and practices of the church. Poignantly mirroring the letter writer's reality, Paul's absence from Ephesus calls for the sending of instructions, and so he establishes Timothy to teach and lead in his stead. The letter is very much an extension of this plan, and provides further instruction and fortification for Timothy in the process of leading the church. Within this framework, the primary content of the first chapter and the entire letter is engaged. The church is in conflict with 'certain people' who teach differently and practise the faith differently than the letter writer would like. Such is the crisis that calls for the present instructions, and to this crisis the letter writer brings heated polemic and swift commands for the organization and administration of the church.

1 Timothy 1.1-2: A greeting to Timothy from Paul

The greeting of the letter is terse, containing the essential information within the form of the ancient Hellenistic letter of sender ('Paul'), and recipient ('Timothy'). That the connection of these parties is grounded in their shared confession in Jesus Christ cannot be in doubt. The title 'Christ Jesus (*christou iesou*)' appears no less than three times in these two slim verses. This order of the title is preferred by the letter writer, but is less common than the reverse presentation *iesou christou* which is seen in the rest of the letters of the Pauline tradition. Such a focus on the confessional formula is characteristic of the opening of other letters in the Pauline tradition (e.g. Rom. 1.1, 1 Cor. 1.1, 2 Cor. 1.1, Phil. 1.1, Eph. 1.1, Col. 1.1), but here the lack of other details makes the centrality of the confession of Jesus Christ all the more stark. The Christocentric focus is further demonstrated by the parallel claims in 1.1 and 1.2: 'Christ Jesus our hope' and 'Christ Jesus our Lord'. These elements make clear that the confession of Christ Jesus shapes the letter writer's theology and eschatology. As the letter unfolds, however, surprisingly little of the contents are concerned with detailed teaching or correction related to belief about Jesus Christ. Rather the vast majority of teaching and correction in the letter is related to particular practices and the social organization of the church, in other words with practical matters. What seems clear from this apparent disparity between the letter's framework and its content is that the letter writer understands that his recipient(s) share a common belief in Christ Jesus that can be assumed and expressed in a formulaic way. It does not have to be set forth in detail or fully explained. Comparatively speaking the content of Paul's teaching about Christ characterized in the Philippian Hymn (Phil. 2.5-11) or the Words of Institution of the Lord's Supper (1 Cor. 11.23-26) is not found within the letter. It would seem that while Paul may have been writing to mixed groups in terms of formation in the Christian traditions, 1 Timothy was intended for those who would know these traditions well and with whom the author of the letter could assume agreement about their basic meaning and purpose. Not only does this distance from the uncontested letters of Paul, it also distances the kind of audience that can generally be presumed within Paul's letters. It is a letter written to church leaders, not to a congregation as a whole. Rather than being addressed to the life of an entire community, it is targeted to a leadership that is understood to be responsible for the daily function- ing of a community. In this sense Paul and Timothy are 'stand ins' for the leadership of the church and their private communication provides important inside information about what the church is and how it should be led.

The first verse of the greeting serves to establish the apostolic authority of Paul: 'Paul an Apostle of Christ Jesus by the command of God our Savior and of Christ Jesus our hope' (NRSV). This introduction is much in keeping with the other letters within the Pauline tradition (e.g. 1 Cor. 1.1, 2 Cor. 1.1, Gal. 1.1, Eph. 1.1, Col. 1.1). By the time of the writing of 1 Timothy a primary characteristic of Paul's legend was that he had been called to be an apostle directly by the will of God. Indeed the greeting sections of the seven uncontested letters of Paul also make such claims (e.g. Rom. 1.1 and Gal. 1.1ff.); however, in these letters other points of identification are also given. In Philippians and Philemon, for example, Paul is a slave of Christ, with no reference to his calling. In 1 Thessalonians Paul simply identifies himself by name. In the Deutero-Pauline and Pastoral Epistle tradition, however, the necessity of identifying Paul as an apostle called by God has taken on a formulaic nature. In this sense the other pseudepigraphical letters seem to present less of the person of Paul and more of a carefully crafted persona about him.

The persona of Paul particularly in relationship to his 'conversion' experience was developed by Luke in his Acts of the Apostles with the threefold repetition of the story of the 'Damascus Road' (Acts 9.1-29, 22.3-21, 26.9-20). In the threefold telling of this tradition Luke underscores that Paul's conversion was Christophanic, consisting of a flash of light and the voice of Jesus calling to him. In addition to this aspect, Luke tells the tradition of Paul's Christophany to dramatize the reversal that Saul, who had been a vicious persecutor of the church, had now become the proclaimer of the gospel to the Gentiles. Luke narrates the tradition of Paul's conversion in a way that underscores his important themes of the sovereignty of God in Jesus Christ and the unity of the church in God's mission in the world. In this sense the persona of 'Paul the converted one' serves Luke's particular ecclesiology and theology.

Paul himself clearly drew on the call aspect of identity in different ways according to the rhetorical purposes of his different letters. For example, the specificity of Paul's apostolic authority in Galatians 1.1 is later illustrated in his apostolic apologia in Galatians 1.11-2.14. The reference in Galatians 1.1 indicates that Paul's authority as an apostle is at issue in the letter. The later defence in Galatians 1.1-2.14 illustrates this fact. In the Deutero-Paulines and the PE, however, the claim to apostolic authority is not so much a rhetorical device in the midst of a particular argument as it is a marker of the identity of Paul. Paul himself in the seven uncontested letters seems to have thought of his revelation from God as being a marker of his own independent authority (in the face of other competing authorities within the church) to proclaim the gospel to the Gentiles. As Paul's authority was established and his persona was developed the later interpreters of Paul de-emphasized his own claims to independent authority and elevated his role within the universal movement of the church and God's sovereign plan for history. The characterization of Paul's calling in 1 Timothy 1.1 is very much in keeping with this later development in the portrayal of Paul in relationship to his calling and to the church.

In addition to establishing the true persona of Paul as God's apostle, the letter's reference to Paul's call sets an important tone for the discourse on power vested in 1 Timothy (and all the PE). This apostle's words can be trusted because they are the words of one who has been commanded by God. This statement about the apostle Paul and his authority to speak infuse the instructions to follow with divine authority.

In 1 Timothy 1.1 the letter writer characterizes Paul's calling with the unusual verb 'command' (*epitage*). This verb underscores the notion of a militarily marshalled force behind the greeting's claim about Paul's call. Interestingly, in the seven uncontested letters of Paul this term does not appear in relationship to Paul's calling. He does use it to refer to God's commands (*epitage*) in Romans 16.26. The use of the term in relationship to God's command of Paul, which underlines his authority as God's agent, does appear in 1 Timothy 1.1, and Titus 1.3. The term announces that the disputations and directions contained in this letter flow directly from one who has been commanded by God. With this introduction, the chain of command is made clear. The letter writer speaks as Paul who has been marshalled by God and who speaks for God. The letter's recipients are informed that their part is to obey the enclosed instructions and to be shaped by these words of Paul to lead and protect the church.

The use of the verb *epitage* in 1 Timothy 1.1 infuses the letter writer's use of language with authority. This infusion serves the writer's purpose of engaging the tradition of Paul and his legacy to do battle with the speech of his opponents. This is merely the first in a string of incidents in which the letter writer asserts what he desires to be true, namely that his speech and the teachings of his church will prevail in the ensuing war of words. The connotations of military force and direct authority available in the verb underscore the desire of the letter writer for a univocal tradition about Paul and a uniform foundation of the church.

In 1 Timothy 1.2 the letter writer moves from describing Paul the sender of the letter to characterizing Timothy the recipient. In this Timothy is described in relation to Paul as a 'legitimate' (*gnesios*) child in the faith (BAGD, 162-3). While the RSV translates the adjective as 'true' child, and the NRSV as 'genuine' child, both miss the sense in which the letter writer is seeking to establish the direct connection between Paul's teaching and Timothy's leadership. This way of naming the recipient continues the powerful construction of the letter's trustworthiness. Again in Titus 1.4 Timothy is named as Paul's 'legitimate (*gnesios*) child in the faith'. This evokes an intimate, paternal connection between the sender and recipient. As Paul is demonstrably connected to God and Christ Jesus by 'command', so too Timothy is connected to Paul as a child to a parent, moreover they (and the potential readers of the letter) are bound to one another in the faith. Importantly the thrust of the term 'legitimate' (*gnesios*) is used in Greek literature for designating children born in wedlock.

This sense of 'legitimacy' with regard to the connection between Paul and Timothy serves to establish an important concern for the letter writer. As there are elements within and without the church that are 'false' and illegitimate, the letter writer is compelled to establish this relationship between Paul and Timothy and their communication as originally and legitimately bound to Paul. At the same time as the letter writer is establishing the intimacy between Paul and Timothy (and thereby the privileged nature of this communication), he is also establishing the purity of line of the teachings that are contained within the letter as those shared between Paul, the father, and his legitimate child, Timothy. This particular construction of the relationship between Paul and Timothy is intended to underscore the doctrinal purity of the communication found in the letter more than it seeks to establish an interpersonal connection between the sender and recipient. Once again, as the letter writer is engaged in a war of words with his opponents about the interpretation of Paul's letters and the life of the church this desire for purity and clarity of speech comes to play an important role. The speech of this letter is 'legitimate' and can be trusted. In contrast the speech of the opponents is 'illegitimate' and must be ignored.

The naming of Timothy, within the pseudepigraphical understanding of the letter, evokes a trusted companion of Paul known throughout the Pauline tradition. Four of Paul's seven undisputed letters name Timothy as a co-sender (1 Thes. 1.1, 2 Cor. 1.1, Phil. 1.1, Philemon 1.1). In the Deutero-Pauline letters the same pair appear (Col. 1.1 and 2 Thess. 1.1). In another of Paul's letters Timothy is mentioned in the closing greetings (e.g. 1 Cor. 16.10-11) as a close companion and co-worker with Paul. While Luke somewhat minimizes Timothy's importance in Paul's ministry (Acts 16ff.), it appears in Paul's epistles as though Timothy was a trusted colleague and emissary to churches (e.g. 1 Cor. 4.17 and Phil. 2.19-24) who stood in Paul's stead to express Paul's pastoral concern and to teach the gospel.

The relationship between Paul and Timothy is evoked in the PE corpus to establish the connection of Paul and a trusted co-worker and friend. In a sense, while the historical Timothy may have stood in for Paul in his ministry among the churches, here the letter to him 'stands in' as a means of keeping churches in line with the writer's understanding of the Pauline tradition. Timothy had been an intermediary player, who ran between Paul and his churches to bear news and establish right teaching and practices. He extended the presence and ministry of Paul where Paul could not be physically present. Just so, this letter written to Timothy functions to bear the teaching of 'Paul' as the letter writer understands him, and to extend Paul's presence and apostolic authority when he can no longer be physically present.

In addition to extending the presence and power of Paul, the construction of a correspondence in which Paul writes directly to Timothy bears the promise of unfettered, forthright, 'inside' information. Paul, who has been called by God, is speaking directly to his most trusted companion, his 'legitimate child in faith', Timothy (one who literally 'honours' or 'fears God'). In this 1 Timothy is constructed in such a way that its author and recipient are fictions in the service of providing a forum for the letter writer to set forth his claims about the church, its practices, its social organization, its offices and its comportment in relation to the larger world.

With the characterizing of the filial relationship between Paul and Timothy the tone for the entire letter has been set in this brief greeting. The letter bears Paul's instruction, without bias or blemish. It comes directly from one called by God, and it is written in utmost confidence to a trusted friend and co-worker who is the 'legitimate' inheritor of Paul's thought. This is as close to the 'true Paul' as one would ever hope to get. Through this introduction and pseudepigraphical device the instructions that follow appear to those who 'overhear' the letter as none other than the direct command of God. If one were invested in the project of correcting or directing the interpretation of the Pauline tradition and legacy within the church, one could not pick a more effective device for the task.

1 Timothy 1.3-11: Warnings against 'other' teachings

After the premise and authority of the letter are established in 1 Timothy 1.1-2, the letter writer does not waste time getting to the heart of the matter. Following the brief opening greeting the letter diverges abruptly into a direct instruction to Timothy regarding the maintenance of the church in Ephesus. The writer discloses that Paul sends these instructions to Ephesus where Timothy has been told to remain for the purposes of commanding 'certain persons' not to teach a different doctrine (*heterodidaskalein*). As noted in the introduction, the place name 'Ephesus' could possibly serve as a generic description of Paul's home base of operation during the writing of the majority of his uncontested letters, or it may establish the provenance of the letter as the region of Asia Minor. Indeed many elements of the contents of the Pastoral Epistles fit well within a late first-century or early second-century CE Asia Minor context. As Bauer and the proponents of his hypothesis, such as Helmut Koester (1965), have established, the region of Asia Minor in the late first and early second centuries CE was rife with conflict regarding the interpretation of Paul and the administration of the church. Valentinus, Marcion and many others had widely assumed the authority of Paul's occasional letters, but had applied them variously to their own contexts, beliefs and practices. In such a climate the definition of 'the gospel' was very much under negotiation. As such the reference to Ephesus both serves to ground the letter within the traditional seat of Paul's work, and to provide a fitting backdrop for the polemic within which the letter writer is about to engage.

In 1 Timothy 1.3 the neologism *heterodidaskalein* is literally translated as 'to teach a different way'. The phrase, used also in 1 Timothy 6.3, seems to echo the astonished claim of Paul in Galatians 1.6 that the Galatian churches (which may have included Ephesus) were so quickly deserting Paul to turn to a different gospel (*heteron euangellion*). Paul, in Galatians, corrects himself immediately to say that of course there is only one gospel, but he goes on to explain that there are those who want to alter the gospel of Christ. This notion of alteration or perversion of the true, pure and unitary is very much at the foreground of 1 Timothy. In this sense, the seemingly casual aside of 1 Timothy 1.3–7 is far from incidental to the letter. It serves to set an agenda for the instructions to follow. As the letter writer sees it, there are 'certain people' in the church who are teaching 'differently'. The goal of the letter is in large part to delineate these people and their different teachings as outside the church and the plan of God, while offering to those who are on the inside (presumably the readers of the letter) the correct teaching of the faith.

From the perspective of historical reconstruction the specifics of the different teachings and the details about just who these 'certain people' may be are frustratingly vague, and the historical reconstruction of their beliefs and practices is extremely elusive. Concern for myths and genealogies could apply widely to many different early Christian (Jewish and Gnostic) interests. Many commentators have settled on some kind of hybrid heretical group to explain these behaviours (e.g. 'Jewish-Christian Gnosticism'). For example, in his commentary on the PE Dibelius notes that it is impossible to identify such a hybrid heresy with any of the Gnostic sects known to us (Dibelius and Conzelmann, 66), yet this does not stop him from identifying the heresy addressed in the Pastorals as a 'Judaizing Gnosticism' (Dibelius and Conzelmann, 65). This combination identification is drawn from other charges in 1 Timothy and the other PE against those who abstain from certain foods and marriage (1 Tim. 4.1-5, 2 Tim. 3.6-9, Tit. 3.9-11). While it is possible that all of these different references point to a general group and their practices, it is problematic to lump them all together in a group so vague that it could fit any Christian expression opposed to the Pastorals' brand of 'orthodoxy'. Such a blanket description is hardly helpful from a historical perspective, and potentially obscures the sharp divisions that the letter writer seems to be drawing between 'legitimate faith' and the beliefs of others. Throughout 1 Timothy there do seem to be elements of Gnostic and mystic religious practice present in the letter writer's critique. In 1 Timothy 4.3-5, for example, the letter writer critiques his opponents for their ascetic practice (abstinence from certain foods and marriage), but, depending on one's reading of 1 Corinthians 7, 1 Corinthians 8-10, and Romans 12, Paul himself could be charged with the same practices.

The letter writer's description of his opponents in 1 Timothy 1.4 as those who 'occupy themselves with endless myths and genealogies' (NRSV), illustrates the difficulty of isolating and defining any particular known Christian practice that one might call 'heretical'. For example, the respective birth narratives of the canonical works of Matthew and Luke could be charged with being 'occupied' with genealogies. In addition, the early Jewish practice of *Midrash* in relation to embellishing the faith of ancestors, and demonstrating the lineage of one community to the history of the past (e.g. Hebrews 11, or *1 QS* 3.13-15) could also be seen in the letter writer's criticisms. That which appears to be defined as the 'true' faith or 'orthodox' tradition to this letter writer seems to have been quite different from the church's process of canonization. In this way, the letter unwittingly bears witness to the diversity of early Christianity evident within the canon itself. Such a witness undermines the letter writer's claim that there is only one true church and one true expression of the faith. It is another case of how the letter writer's war of words on subversive speech is very much doomed from the beginning. Underneath the voice of his ongoing insistence on the singular purity of the church there is a quiet voice asking: 'if the church is unified why are there so many other teachings and other ways of being the church to be combated?'

In contrast to the activities of myths and genealogies, whatever they may have represented historically speaking, the letter writer holds up divine training (*oikonomian*) which is in faith. The goal of such instruction according to the letter writer is love that comes from a pure heart, a right conscience and a sincere faith. These instructions appear as circular platitudes: divine training in one's faith has the goal of love that emerges from sincere faith. These virtuous goals are held up against the activities of those whom the letter writer notes have 'deviated' from the faith.

The letter writer describes the practices of the errant people in the realm of teaching in a way that underscores his preoccupation with speech. According to him, these different teachers speak without meaning (1.6, *mataiologian*), they speak without understanding (1.7), they do not know what they are saying, and they make vain assertions (1.7). Once again, words, their trustworthiness, immutability and purity, are at issue for the letter writer. While the greeting and instructions to Timothy have been preoccupied with demonstrating the reliability of the letter's teaching, the words of those who would 'desire to be teachers of the law' are characterized as singularly untrustworthy. The lines are clear. This is a context of dire struggle for the letter writer. The goal is the preservation of his understanding of the truth against all those voices and forces that would seek to change it. And yet, both the letter writer and those he would seek to discredit have words with which to teach. The problem then for the letter writer is establishing that his words are the 'right' words.

The project of establishing the reliability of one's own teaching, one's own words, while discrediting the teaching and words of another is a difficult task. It is one word against another. Discrediting the words of one's opponents as 'false' is particularly challenging when one is engaged in a pseudepigraphical deception. Seen through the lens of pseudepigraphy, the letter writer's protest that these 'others' pose falsely as teachers of the law has the feel of 'the pot calling the kettle black'. In such a context words are both the ammunition and the armour. While such an observation may mitigate the letter writer's claims to the 'pure faith', it also builds some empathy for his situation. When one understands the context of the letter as a part of a rhetorical battle for Paul's legacy, the claims regarding sound doctrine and correct teaching can be seen not so much as a description of the church as it was, but rather as prescriptive language in a struggle to move the church in a particular direction. When the PE writer is viewed in this light, whether or not interpreters agree with his particular ecclesiology, he must be appreciated as an innovator in the life of the early church. While the PE writer's vision of the church occupies an extremely privileged position in its current canonical location, historically speaking his voice represents one claim among many about what Paul intended for the church and how the church is to live in the world.

The notion of a central, pure teaching is once again underscored by the letter writer's references to the law in 1 Timothy 1.7. Here the letter writer characterizes those who desire to be teachers of the law. According to the writer, the law is not the problem. It is good as long as it is used lawfully. For the writer this means that it is applied not to the righteous (one would assume this includes him and his community), but to the lawless. At this point, a stock vice list appears defining just who the lawless are (which may well include the opponents who identify themselves as 'teachers of the law'). All of these enemies, ranging in their sins from murder, to sexual immorality, to slave trade, to perjury promote whatever is contrary to 'sound teaching'. With this final claim the letter writer returns to his core subject, correct teaching. This in turn brings him to the constructed subject of Paul who is the authority commanded by God to guard the gospel (*ho episteuthen ego*, 1 Tim. 1.11). Remarkably Paul has been transformed in this construction from one who proclaims the gospel (as he states throughout his own letters), to one who guards it.

As a whole the section of 1 Timothy 1.3-11 forms an inclusio with the greeting in 1 Timothy 1.1-2. It returns the reader to the source, and therefore the trustworthiness of this teaching: the gospel of God which God entrusted to Paul (1 Tim. 1.11, NRSV). More than simply emphasizing the authority of Paul's and therefore the letter writer's teaching, however, the section of 1 Timothy 1.3-11 has set the stage for the war of words. The letter writer has introduced the context of struggle into which these instructions are delivered. The readers of the letter have been apprised. There are sides to choose in the letter writer's vision of the faith and, as progeny of Timothy, Paul's true child in the faith, the readers of the letter have been prepared to reject what is 'meaningless talk' and to choose what is genuine. What the letter writer has unintentionally revealed, however, in the discourse of the letter is that he protests too much. As noted above, there is a tension inherent within the project of rhetorically attacking the speech of others. If the teachings of those who swerve from the truth are vain, empty and meaningless why do they need to be challenged? If the faith the letter writer espouses is genuine why does it need to be so vigorously defended? The war of words is on, and the letter's reader is engaged to choose the right side in the battle.

1 Timothy 1.12-17: Paul's personal example of God's mercy in Christ

At this point the letter returns to a more conventional epistolary form and the letter writer inserts the anticipated thanksgiving. Normally, the thanksgiving would immediately follow the greeting of the letter. The seven uncontested letters demonstrate Paul's agile placement of this form for rhetorical effect. In Philippians, for example, he offers an extremely protracted thanksgiving, while in Galatians he omits the section altogether. In 1 Timothy the thanksgiving is misplaced, and though quite long, has the rhetorical agenda (much as the brief greeting in 1.1-2) of establishing and drawing upon the legend and personality of Paul.

In the uncontested letters Paul uses the thanksgiving form to establish his relationships with those to whom he is writing. He often gives thanks for the church (e.g. Phil. 1.3ff.), and he gives thanks for those to whom he is writing (e.g. Philemon 4-5). In 1 Timothy 1.12-17, however, the letter writer does not give thanks for the church in Ephesus, nor for Timothy. Rather he portrays Paul giving thanks to Christ for Paul's conversion and his apostolic calling. Such a projection of Paul's biography offers the letter writer another opportunity to ground his instruction within genuine Pauline tradition, and yet direct that tradition toward his purposes. As such, it is clear that 1 Timothy does not seek to establish relationships with a church or a leader so much as it seeks to portray its authenticity within the Pauline legacy.

As known from extant canonical sources such as Galatians 1.13 and Acts 8.3, prior to his conversion, Paul was a notable opponent of the church who then through the grace of God received his conversion and call. It is on the point of grace, however, that the letter writer of 1 Timothy, though citing Pauline tradition, seems to deviate from the anticipated Pauline pattern of thought. As expected, the letter writer states that he ('Paul') blasphemed, persecuted and acted arrogantly. This is in keeping with Paul's own description of his 'earlier life' prior to conversion (e.g. Gal. 1.13, Phil. 3.6, 1 Cor. 15.9). In these references, Paul understands his conversion to have cosmological and theological significance. It is a demonstration of God's grace. For example, in Galatians 1.13 Paul notes that his conversion is not so much an act of Christ's mercy, as it is one of divine providence. He understands in Galatians 1.15 that he was set apart for this conversion when he was in his mother's womb, and in Galatians 1.23 he notes that his conversion has become known in the churches of Judaea as evidence for the glory of God in Christ: 'He who persecuted us is now preaching the faith he once tried to destroy.'

In 1 Timothy 1.13 note that the letter writer claims that Paul received 'Christ's mercy' because he persecuted the church out of ignorance and in unbelief. However, in 1 Timothy 1.12-17, Paul's conversion takes on a different purpose. This is an example of Christ's personal mercy to Paul, not divine providence in general. It has individual rather than cosmological significance. The experience of mercy is recounted to illumine Paul's exemplary biography more than it makes a theological claim. In 1 Timothy Paul is an example of how a sinner can be saved. As foremost among sinners (1 Tim. 1.15, contrast with 1 Cor. 15.9), he has received mercy so that he might be an example of Christ's infinite patience. The object for the letter writer is to move people from ignorance and unbelief to faith. Paul did this, and has inherited eternal life. The letter writer holds out that same hope for those who are in his churches. Behind this hope, however, there lingers the real danger of wrong belief and its consequence of ultimate damnation.

The use of Paul's personal example is significant in the letter. In the seven uncontested letters Paul holds himself up as an example, as someone to be imitated as he has attempted to imitate Christ (1 Cor. 11.1). The goal for Paul is to build his churches into greater conformity with Christ, to be 'the body of Christ' (e.g. 1 Cor. 12 and Rom. 12). In his suffering, patience and humility Paul calls his communities to imitate him. In this sense of imitation Paul understands his conversion and call as part of his understanding of God's work in Jesus Christ: the dead are made alive, the Jew and Greek are made one, the persecutor has become the proclaimer. In 1 Timothy 1.12-17, however, the paradigm makes a shift. Paul's conversion is focused on Paul himself. He becomes the historical example of a converted former blasphemer. The lesson of this paradigm is Christ's patience and mercy. The purpose has become the attraction of believers. The focus on the corporate goal of the 'body of Christ' seen in 1 Corinthians 12 and Romans 12 has shifted to the saved individual, who is the recipient of Christ's mercy. This subtle shift is 'Pauline' only in its use of Paul's name and legend, but it anticipates a very non-Pauline ethic and model of the church. In his uncontested letters Paul proclaims the corporate nature of salvation within the church as the body of Christ. Therefore it is ironic that here in 1 Timothy he is held up as a model of one who has individually received the mercy of Christ and who holds out that hope to other individuals.

The personal example of Paul and the mediation of Christ's mercy is concluded in 1 Timothy 1.17 with a traditional Jewish doxology. For the letter writer, who later in 1 Timothy 2.5-7 will meld this Jewish confession with a Christological formula, this does not constitute a change of focus. It is an example of how the letter writer incorporates previously existing forms into the fabric of the letter. It also provides an opportunity to authorize the prior appropriation of Paul as a model of Christ's mercy and right belief with a standard confessional trumpet blast. The Jewish pietistic affirmations of God's kingship, eternity and singularity evoke a helpful standard for the letter writer's programme of establishing genuine belief. The doxological formula implies a rock-solid foundation, as old as the ages, that will endure forever. It is upon this kind of rock that this letter writer is desperately trying to build and fortify the church.

1 Timothy 1.18-20: A charge to Timothy with a warning

From the eternity of the ages and God's kingship the letter writer returns in 1 Timothy 1.18-20 to address Timothy directly. After this section, the second-person recipient will not be evoked again until 1 Timothy 3.14-16. In these final verses of the first chapter the subject returns, much as in the prior direct address to Timothy in 1.8-11, to the project of maintaining genuine faith in the face of opponents.

The charge laid before Timothy by the letter writer is drawn into a larger scope by evoking the event of Timothy's 'call' or ordination in service with Paul. The difficult phrase 'in accordance with prophetic utterances which pointed to you' (*kata tas progousas epi se profeteias*) most probably refers to a liturgical event in which Timothy, either by Paul or other leaders, was set aside and designated for his service in the church (Quinn and Wacker, 150). This service of Timothy's ordination is further referenced in 1 Timothy 4.4 and 2 Timothy 1.6. The function of this reminiscence is to combine the letter writer's authority to instruct Timothy with the authority of the Spirit through which the original prophecies were made. In this sense the letter writer attempts to align his voice and instruction with the purposes of God.

The event of prophetic utterance to which the letter writer refers in 1 Timothy 1.18 upholds the authority of prophetic utterance in much the way Paul affirms the gift of prophetic speech over the gift of ecstatic speech or 'tongues' (*glossai*) in 1 Corinthians 14.1-5. For Paul prophetic speech was composed of proclamation about God for the instruction of people. According to Paul in 1 Corinthians 14 it serves an important purpose of consolation and encouragement. In 1 Timothy

1.18 'prophetic speech' is understood to be a vehicle through which the church leadership discerns those who are called out to serve, as in the case of Timothy. In this development what was for Paul a particular gift of being in the Spirit of Christ (set alongside other such gifts) seems to become a particular medium of the church's discernment and practice of selecting and authorizing its own leadership.

The purposes of those original declarations of prophetic utterance to Timothy were, according to the letter writer, to inspire Timothy that he 'fight the good fight' (1 Tim. 1.18, NRSV) in delineating genuine faith from what is false. Importantly the letter writer uses a related verb and noun to characterize the empowerment of Timothy from his prophetic speech. The verb is *strateuo* and the noun is *strateia*. Both terms relate to the notion of military campaign and service. The NRSV translates the first phrase 'so that following them you may *wage* the good warfare'. The translation misses the military emphasis of the verb. A better translation might read: 'that *marshalled* by them you might fight the good fight'. Seen in this way, the letter writer imagines that Timothy has been infused with the posture of battle through these prophetic utterances, and that through this infusion he will be filled with the power to wage war against all falsehood in the church. By using this military strategic imagery the letter writer evokes the manner in which he described the calling of Paul by God in 1 Timothy 1.1 as a command (*epitagen*). In this sense Timothy's designation by the church leadership is held together with Paul's calling by God to be an apostle. They are both warriors in a battle waged by God on behalf of the true faith and the true church.

As noted above, the term *strateian* evokes a military campaign. This sensibility of struggle is employed by Paul in the use of athletic imagery in texts such as 1 Corinthians 9.25 and Philippians 3.14. In 1 Timothy 1.18 what had been Paul's struggle is bestowed upon Timothy, and the recipients of the letter, but the goal of that struggle is somewhat different. Paul's references to struggle refer to the work of 'saving some' (1 Cor. 9.25) or pressing on to the goal of perfection in Christ (Phil. 3.12-16). The claim in 1 Timothy 1.18, on the other hand, is a struggle against that doctrine which is false. By placing the struggle and the rightness of the cause within the context of Timothy's original calling the letter writer accomplishes the placement of the current struggles of the church into the realm of ultimate significance. Timothy's selection to church leadership was imbued with the call of prophetic utterance that has equipped him, according to the letter writer, not with the authority to save souls or to preach the gospel, but to discern what is false from what is true. The struggle that the letter writer describes resonates with the larger pattern of his rhetoric throughout the writing. In all of this, the church envisioned by the letter writer is not so much an agent of the good news among the Gentiles or throughout the world as it is a fortress in the fight for right doctrine, and the protection of 'genuine' belief.

In 1 Timothy 1.19, 20, as in 1 Timothy 1.6-7, the activities of those whom the letter writer deems the enemies in this struggle are difficult to discern from a historical perspective. Earlier in 1 Timothy 1.5 the letter writer characterizes his goal for the church as 'good conscience', and 'genuine faith'. In 1 Timothy 1.19 Timothy is charged to hold faith and 'good conscience' and reminded that there are those who have rejected this path and have thereby 'made shipwreck' (*enauagesan*) of their faith. The verb 'shipwreck' (*naugageo*) is one Paul employs, but only in the literal sense to refer to actual shipwrecks he had endured (2 Cor. 11.25). The metaphorical use of shipwreck is extremely poetic and can be found in the allegorical writings of Philo of Alexandria (e.g. *Mut. Nom.* 215, and *Somn. 2*, 147, cited in BAGD, 534). The dramatic flair of the notion of 'making shipwreck' of one's faith bespeaks the sense of disaster that departing from truth and sound teaching holds for the letter writer. The peril surrounding the recipients of the letter in their journey of ministry is boldly coloured in the use of this metaphor. Importantly, the disaster seems first to befall individuals who the writer describes as having made a 'shipwreck of *their* faith'. In other words, the peril that the letter writer fights is first and foremost the spiritual destruction of individuals in the church. From this emphasis it is clear that the letter writer understands that the faith and practice of each individual member of the church is essential to maintain in order to ensure the strength of the whole.

The historical particularities regarding what the letter writer's opponents have done are elusive. The images of 'having conscience', 'rejecting conscience' (NRSV), and the contrast of the letter writer's vision for the church with the image of a shipwreck, are instructive. According to the letter writer, the church is on a treacherous course. Loss of control regarding its central tenets such as faith and good conscience (however those might be defined) will result not simply in the loss of faith, but in institutional disaster. From the letter writer's perspective, this disaster is made up of the loss of individual members who both lead and are led astray.

The noun *suneidesis* which the NRSV translates as 'conscience' is used throughout the NT literature to denote 'awareness' on both a moral and spiritual level (BAGD, 787). The letter writer employs the term in 1 Timothy 1.19 to denote a state of mind and spirit that is immoveable in relation to the teachings of opponents. Good conscience, in other words, is a state of mind and spirit that agrees with the teaching of the letter writer, and loss of conscience would be a perspective that follows after other teachings and other teachers.

In 1 Timothy 1.20 the letter writer specifically names some of 'these certain (*tines*) people who have revoked their "good conscience" ', and followed other teachings. Hymenaus and Alexander are lifted up as negative examples. The specifics of how they have rejected conscience are not named. Apparently the letter writer is confident that his audience is aware of their situation and the mere mention of their names will evoke for his readers the scandal of their actions, but his description that they have 'rejected' good conscience implies that at one time Hymenaus and Alexander possessed good conscience. Their case, as such, would contrast with the prior example of Paul before his call and conversion (discussed in 1 Tim. 1.12-17). Paul received Christ's mercy, according to the letter writer, because he was ignorant and unbelieving. On the contrary, Hymenaeus and Alexander are not deserving of such mercy. They had at one time correct faith, and now they have rejected it. In due course, therefore, the letter writer announces their paradigmatic fate. They have been handed over to Satan in order to be taught (*paideuthosin*) not to blaspheme. While their situation seems bleak, the notion that they might yet be taught (*paideuthosin*) does offer at least a glimmer of the possibility of their redemption and inclusion back into the church.

In this final almost fanciful claim about the delivery of Hymenaeus and Alexander to Satan, the letter writer puts forth two important ideas. The first is that the offence of Hymenaeus and Alexander is related to wrong speech. In other words, they have blasphemed. In keeping with the central issues the letter writer seeks to combat, the blasphemy of Hymenaeus and Alexander has resulted in their apparent expulsion from the church. In this way the letter writer underscores his intolerance of speech that disagrees with his teaching and sends an important message about the consequences of such speech to his readers. The second important idea which the letter writer conveys in this section about the particular misdeeds and ill fate of two people is that through their example he is able to reaffirm the theological claim made earlier in the doxological formula in 1 Timothy 1.17: 'To the King of ages, immortal, invisible, the only God, be honor and glory for ever and ever. Amen' (NRSV). God indeed is immortal and invisible, and due all glory for all eternity, because within the letter writer's theological system even Satan can be marshalled for the purposes of teaching right doctrine. Such a bold claim about God's sovereign presence and power can be found also within Israel's wisdom traditions. Indeed in the book of Job God and Satan interact to test the extent of Job's fear of God and the depth of his piety (Job 1.6-12). In the context of 1 Timothy the claim about Satan's pedagogical value for Hymenaeus and Alexander seems ultimately to express the letter writer's convictions about the sovereignty of God. Finally, such a claim puts the letter writer in his purpose to defend the true faith in full command of the powers of heaven and hell. Note in 1 Timothy 1.20 that letter writer claims that he has 'turned over' (*paradidomi*) Hymenaeus and Alexander to Satan that they might learn not to blaspheme. As such the letter writer is actively involved in determining who is saved and who is damned. Importantly, such power for the letter writer's pedagogy does not stop with Hymenaeus and Alexander alone (who are themselves perhaps not yet beyond redemption), but includes those who would hear and read the letter as well.

As is often the case throughout 1 Timothy, the letter writer in 1 Timothy 1.20 engages an apparently particular and ostensibly insignificant detail out of daily church life to make a grand theological claim. Even those, such as Hymenaeus and Alexander, who seek to thwart the truth and subvert the church are ultimately within the reach of God's sovereign purposes. They can function as negative examples or by their instruction from Satan may even return to the church and bear witness to God's redemptive power. Such insight into the sovereign and mysterious purposes of God is gained from one who assumes the posture of a true 'overseer' (*episkopos*) of the church. From his supervisory vantage point the letter writer can see all contingencies in the church. In his letter he seeks to develop this capacity for such oversight in those who read his letter and would lead his church.

1 Timothy 2.1-3.13:
Ordering the Community

Introduction

As a unit the large section of 1 Timothy 2.1-3.13 contains no direct second-person address to Timothy. The absence of such address, however, does not mean that the unit is free of instruction. It is full of imperatives from the letter writer (e.g. 'I exhort', 'I desire', 'A bishop must', 'deacons must', etc.) directed ostensibly to the leadership of the church in general. The directives from the letter writer in this section concern primarily the practices and offices of the church. 1 Timothy 2.1-7 takes up the activity of prayers offered on behalf of secular leaders, 1 Timothy 2.8-15 deals with the activity of prayer in the church by men and women, and 1 Timothy 3.1-13 offers instructions regarding the qualifications and comportment for the offices of bishop and deacon. In general the contents seem to assume that the recipients of this information have oversight of these practices, and that they occupy leadership positions within the church.

The material contained in this central portion of the letter bears none of the overt signs of controversy in the church witnessed in the previous direct address to Timothy in 1.6ff. and 1.18-20. Yet not far below the surface the injunctions for prayers on behalf of leaders in high secular positions, for women's silence and submission, and for the sobriety of church leaders may be evidence of trouble. In a between-the-lines reading might these injunctions be a witness to those who refuse to recognize secular authority, women who assume the privilege to pray, teach and preach, and deacons and bishops who do not conform to the letter writer's ideal of piety? The rhetoric of this section is not directly confrontational, but it suggests that the letter writer is embroiled in controversies about these very issues, and employs the venue of a long lost, intimate correspondence between Paul and his trusted lieutenant Timothy in order to insist on an original, singular and true way of being church. Indeed this very venue ensures the letter writer of the opportunity of describing this church and its practices in a ruse that assumes perfect agreement between sender and recipient. Of course 'Paul' and 'Timothy' agree on these things! These are the activities of a well-ordered, godly and faithful church, the church they founded together. Such an idealized construction upholds the singularity of the letter writer's understanding of the church, and discredits the understandings of all those who would hold to a different view.

1 Timothy 2.1-7: Prayers on behalf of secular leaders

The first verse of the unit lists four related liturgical activities (entreaties, prayers, intercessions and thanksgivings). The list gives evidence of both a previously existing benedictory formula from early synagogue worship and of table blessings from within early Jewish Christian liturgies (Quinn and Wacker, 172-75). As such, the corporate and private prayers called for here are commanded on behalf of all people. Such an expression envisions the work of the church in its worship and private piety quite differently from Paul's expressions about worship in the seven uncontested letters. Prayer with such a global consciousness is not envisioned in Paul. As Paul requests prayer and writes of having received prayer, it is generally on behalf of his particular ministry (e.g. Phil. 1.9), or the people in his congregations. In 1 Timothy prayer is conceived as less personal and more on behalf of an already established global conception of the church which has concern for 'all people'. Significantly, a church that can understand itself as praying for *all* people is a church that is not concerned with establishing new relationships between specific constituencies of people (e.g. Jews and Gentiles). It may represent a church with a conception of having that goal already somewhat in hand.

The next clause adds specificity to the global expanse of 'all people', with the delineation 'for kings and all who are in positions of authority'. This call for prayer evokes Paul's injunction for subjection to governing authorities in Romans 13.1-7. In both Romans 13.1-7 and 1 Timothy theological justification is given for the relation of the church to governing authorities. This justification is grounded in the view that God alone is sovereign, and as such even secular authority is under God's command. Therefore prayer for and service to the state is prayer for and service to God. Romans 13.1-7 and 1 Timothy 2.1-7 differ remarkably, however, in that Romans 13.1-7 calls for political subjection to the state, whereas in 1 Timothy the letter writer commands corporate prayer on behalf of those who lead in the state. What might such a shift into the interior life of the church, namely its worship, represent?

While the exhortation to be subject to governing authorities in Romans 13 may be attributed to public relations with the state on behalf of the church, in 1 Timothy the letter writer has the interior life of the community, its worship, in view. To this end the clause in 1 Timothy 2.4 offers some clarity. The letter writer affirms the sovereignty of God, and then makes a missiological claim: 'God who is sovereign desires all people to be saved and to come to knowledge of truth.' With the return to the category of 'all people' the letter writer encompasses the specified kings and authorities into the saving plan of God. This claim on the part of the letter writer envisions a scenario in which government officials are not merely a part of the constellation of power under the ultimate control of divine sovereignty (in an eschatological sense). Rather, the letter writer imagines that the interior life of the church, its prayer, is inclusive of concern, praise and thanksgiving for such officials. Perhaps what is indicated here is a situation in which such high officials are a part of that interior life in the fellowship of those who are considered to be saved.

The purpose clause in 1 Timothy 2.2 discloses a very particular vision of the final goal of the church. The subjunctive mood of the verb is instructive in discerning this goal. The letter writer states that the community is to pray for leaders in secular authority 'in order (*hina*) that we *might* lead (*diagomen*) a tranquil and quiet life'. The subjunctive mood of the verb seems to suggest that while such a life is ideal, it is not yet entirely in hand. In the formulation of the letter writer the tranquil life is more of a desire than a reality. It is a hoped-for condition contingent upon the obedience of those who read these instructions.

With the use of the term life (*bion*) the letter writer further identifies his location, particularly within relationship to the uncontested writings of Paul. As the term is used here and in 2 Timothy 2.4 it connotes the notion of everyday private life, or the manner of life for an individual. Importantly this term for life does not appear in Paul's uncontested writings, where the notion of life is conveyed with the more theologically and cosmologically imbued term *zoe*. Life, imagined in the seven uncontested letters of Paul, is life in the Spirit, or life within the larger life of God. Here in 1 Timothy 2.2 the notion of individual lifestyle – in the manner of piety, propriety and respectability – is evoked. The letter writer sees this as pleasing to God (1 Timothy 2.3), but it is not connected to the community's corporate experience within a notion of the life of God's Spirit. As much as corporate prayer is evoked as a realm for upholding governing authorities, the letter writer emphasizes that the goal of all of this activity is to bring about a tranquil private, individual life.

In 1 Timothy 2.5 the letter writer provides his theological justification for the objects and patterns of prayer he has presented in the previous verses. This justification picks up on the notion of one God made earlier in the doxology of 1 Timothy 1.17. There is one God, and one mediator (*mesites*) between God and persons, namely the human Jesus Christ. Here the letter writer employs a previously existing form to enforce the

Christological claim that Jesus Christ mediates between the divine and human precisely because he was human. The function of mediator, particularly in the context of prayer on behalf of governing authorities, would seem to convey the notion of acting as a messenger. As such, Jesus would be envisioned as a bearer of God's message to humans, and likewise of humans to God (Quinn and Wacker, 187). The next phrase of the confession, however, introduces the sacrificial aspect of Christ's death, claiming that he gave his life as a ransom for all (1 Tim. 2.6). Present here are a variety of Christological claims about the saving work of God in Christ as it was variously understood in the early church. As mediator Christ is conveyor of divine wisdom, proclaimer of divine rule. As ransom he is sacrifice, expiation for human sin and protection from divine wrath. In either case, the Christological technicalities of the confession do not appear to be pressing for the letter writer. He is writing instructions for church order and practice, not doctrine. The various confessional claims fit his bill because they proclaim the sovereignty of God (encompassing secular ruling authorities), establish divine precedent for the role of governing authorities as mediators, and include the divine project of saving all people (including kings and governing authorities) in the ancient confession that Christ's death was a 'ransom for all' (see parallels in Mk 10.44, 'for many', Rom. 8.32 and 2 Cor. 5.14-15).

To conclude the exhortation the letter writer returns, once again, to the biographical example of Paul. He is the proclaimer and apostle to the Gentiles. In this description the reader is reminded of Paul's calling to teach the Gentiles in faith and truth. In the midst of this bold self-declaration the letter writer inserts a parenthetical aside: 'I speak the truth, I do not lie.' While many commentators have interpreted this phrase in relation to Paul's own improbable conversion, a kind of 'believe it or not, it's true', the phrase can also be interpreted as a rhetorical move by the letter writer to reassert the veracity and reliability of the letter's directions. Viewed this way and coupled with the return to Paul's call as preacher and apostle, the phrase underscores the prior injunction to pray on behalf of governing authorities with a final claim to authenticity. Moreover, it serves to introduce and embolden the upcoming stipulations regarding men and women's roles in worship. Both exhortations in 1 Timothy 2.1ff. and 2.8ff., then, are tied by the letter writer to the personal example and thereby the authority of Paul. The readers of the letter are instructed through this construction as to their role; they are to believe and follow what the letter writer says.

1 Timothy 2.8-15: Men and women

In this unit the letter writer makes claims that have had far-reaching consequences in the history of the church with regard to the organization of church life and worship, and the role of women within both ecclesial and secular leadership. As these claims have been applied directly as doctrine, complete with their particular theological and hermeneutical justification from Genesis 2-3, they have wielded immense power both over the past two millennia and on a global scale. Whatever aim the letter writer may have had in presenting these proscriptions against women's activity, he could hardly have imagined the reach and effects that his words would have in the history of the church and in many different human cultures.

Early church battles over the role of women in church leadership and life show clearly the influence of 1 Timothy 2.8-15 on what became the orthodox position. Subsequently, the writings of Augustine and later medieval church leaders show a dependence on this text in dealing with subjects ranging from church leadership to decrying the role of women in 'the Fall'. The effect of such rhetoric has been both the limitation of women's political power throughout Christendom and the perpetuation and legitimation of the hatred of women in the guise of maintaining the true church and the proclamation of the gospel.

In the life of the church in the nineteenth and twentieth centuries 1 Timothy 2.8-15 occupied a front line in the defence against the battle for women's suffrage and full participation in church life. In both British and North American history the suffrage workers often found that clergy formed the bastions of protection of male supremacy over women. These clergy legitimized their position with their interpretation of texts such as 1 Timothy 2.8-15. For this reason, a new evaluation of the text was necessary. These new interpreters, motivated by their political goals, were among the first to challenge the authority of 1 Timothy as genuinely Pauline, and argued that its exegesis of Genesis 2-3 was flawed. Such forthright challenges to the interpretive claims of women's subordination to men in 1 Timothy 2 began movements within various denominations to extend the rite of ordination to women. Indeed by the middle of the twentieth century the main-line Congregational, Presbyterian, Episcopalian and Methodist denominations approved women's ordination to the office of pastor or priest.

Despite these movements, contemporary polities of various other churches continue to draw on the text of 1 Timothy 2.8-15 to defend their practices of prohibiting women from serving in the roles of pastor and or priest. For example, the statement of the Lutheran Church, Missouri Synod entitled 'Women in the Church: Scriptural Principles and Ecclesial Practice' claims:

> The theological matrix for the apostle's inspired teaching on the silence of women in the church and the exercise of authority is, again, the order of creation. In 1 Timothy 2.13 Paul points to the order of creation as the basis for the instructions given in verses 11 and 12. God made Adam before Eve; that is, He created man and woman in a definite order. Turning from the creation to the fall, Paul adds that Adam was not deceived but that the woman was deceived and became a transgressor. The conclusion drawn is that the leadership of the official, public teaching office belongs to men. Assumption of that office by a woman is out of place because it is a woman who assumes it, not because women do it in the wrong way or have inferior gifts and abilities.

The Lutheran Church, Missouri Synod is careful to attempt to nuance the offence of 1 Timothy 2.8-15. The church's interpretation states that women are not necessarily inferior as people to do the task of pastoral ministry. Their problem simply is an ontological one – they are women. Women qua women are by nature, by God's design, not fit for the service of the pastoral office. This is not their fault (and here the Lutherans depart from the PE writer); it is simply a part of the inescapable nature of what it means to be a woman. From this contorted hermeneutical effort regarding 1 Timothy 2.8-15 the statement goes on to offer a principle of women's roles in the church:

> The creational pattern of male headship requires that women not hold the formal position of the authoritative public teaching office in the church, that is, in the office of pastor.

What is most alarming about the Lutheran Church, Missouri Synod's statement is the extent to which it seems to want to soften the harshness of the 1 Timothy text, and yet wholly repeats its tacit assumption that Eve was 'transgressor', and that her sin was prototypical of the propensity of all women to sin. It is not that women have inferior gifts, they just suffer from this endemic quality of transgression! The 'creational pattern of male headship' is underlined with the 'creational pattern' of female transgression. God designed it so that women simply cannot hold the 'formal' position of pastor. This formal position itself is apparently knit into the creational pattern, and women simply have not been designed to fill the job. The text of 1 Timothy 2.8-15 lives in the Lutheran Church, Missouri Synod both to define what is essentially feminine and to prohibit the ability of women to serve as official pastors within the church. Clearly 1 Timothy 2.8–15 has been granted a life that continues to affect the lives of women and men within the Lutheran Church, Missouri Synod.

Another example of the reach of the language of 1 Timothy 2.8–15 in the life of contemporary churches may be found in the controversial 'Baptist Faith and Message' statement adopted by the Southern Baptist Convention on 14 June 2000. In this statement, the text of 1 Timothy 2.9–14 is cited as the authority for that denomination's prohibition against women's pastoral leadership. What is perhaps most stunning about the statement is its brevity, and the sense in which the text from 1 Timothy has curtailed women's roles as part of the essential definition of what makes the church the church. In a sense, the PE writer's injunctions for women's silence have been engaged as normative of the 'New Testament church' without any reference to other evidence of women's church leadership found in the Gospels and Acts, the letters of Paul, or other early Christian texts.

> A New Testament church of the Lord Jesus Christ is an autonomous local congregation of baptized believers, associated by covenant in the faith and fellowship of the gospel; observing the two ordinances of Christ, governed by His laws, exercising the gifts, rights, and privileges invested in them by His Word, and seeking to extend the gospel to the ends of the earth. Each congregation operates under the Lordship of Christ through democratic processes. In such a congregation each member is responsible and accountable to Christ as Lord. Its scriptural officers are pastors and deacons. *While both men and women are gifted for service in the church, the office of pastor is limited to men as qualified by Scripture.*
>
> The New Testament speaks also of the church as the Body of Christ, which includes all of the redeemed of all the ages, believers from every tribe, and tongue, and people, and nation. [Emphasis mine to indicate the relevant part of the text referring to 1 Timothy 2.9–14]

The extent to which 1 Timothy concerns itself with the definition of what is 'true' church has clearly supplemented the force of the letter writer's injunctions about women's roles within the community of faith. In both ancient and contemporary polities the debate over women in leadership has been seen as defining what makes the church the church. In this sense, critical interpretation of the text in terms of its historical, social and cultural context is essential in determining what it may have meant for the letter writer's community to enjoin women to silence, and thereby determine what such a claim might mean in contemporary manifestations of the church.

1 Timothy 2.8–15 begins with a reference to men (*andras*) and a direction regarding their practice of prayer. Such a specific reference

to men in prayer would anticipate a parallel reference to women's activity in prayer. In this sense the protracted treatment of women in 1 Timothy 2.9-15, and the lack of any reference to their activity of prayer is surprising. Instead the writer takes issue with the apparel of women (without any reference to liturgical specifics), and the general demeanour of women in public and private life. The letter writer's use of 'likewise' (*hosautos*) to coordinate the men's directions in verse 8 with the women's directions in verses 9-12 artificially joins the two sets of instructions. While both groups are commanded to complete obedience in their behaviour, there is little similarity in what they are expected to do and the contexts in which those expectations are held.

What is the nature of this community of men and women that the writer envisions? Men are called to be in fervent prayer (*boulomai*) in all places (*en panti topo*). Women are called to learn in silence with all submissiveness (*en pase apotage*). The totality of these directions seems to place them more within the realm of a utopian desire rather than an established fact. These directions are, as in other parts of the letter, presented as a kind of ideal. For the letter writer the roles of men and women are clear. The construct of the letter writer's 'Paul' has an ideal authority to prescribe the activities of men and women in all ways.

Keeping the context of the letter's writing in view, it is important to understand that such a prescription for ideal behaviour among men and women did not arise in a vacuum. Rhetorically speaking, these claims regarding behaviour are the letter writer's response to what he considered other, less desirable behaviour. The prayers of some men may have been less pacific (presumably *with* anger and debate). The comportment of some women may have been less than decorous or submissive to authority. A reading-between-the-lines interpretation of the text understands the injunctions to have arisen from a context of much discordant speech on the part of both men and women. It is to such a contentious audience, then, that this particular vision of the church's life is presented as a desire. To assume that such neat divisions between men and women's activities ever held sway is to misunderstand the rhetorical nature and context of the writing. Likewise to accept that the letter writer received the complete level of compliance he demands (*all* places, *all* times) is to ignore that the letter writer is engaged in a battle for influence and control with certain men and women in the church's life. On the other hand, appreciating the section's rhetorical power offers a means of participating in the debate about the nature of human social relationships in the church, and thereby enlivening the text of 1 Timothy 2.8-15 in a way that is in tune with its original context and purposes. By no means does this mean blindly obeying the voice of the letter writer. Rather it means seeing that his instructions represent the voice of a single perspective that evokes other voices of challenge and dissent.

1 Timothy 2.8 addresses the comportment of men in prayer. The first phrase demands that men pray in every place (*en panti topo*). The phrase is likely echoed from the LXX version of Mal. 1.11: 'From the rising to the going down of the sun my name has been glorified among the Gentiles, in every place (*en panti topo*) incense is offered in my name ...' In this light the direction does not indicate that men should pray in such a formal way at all times and in all places, but rather that the comportment of men in prayer in all places of worship should be without argument (see Quinn and Wacker, 209, Bassler, 57). The letter writer's direction clearly represents the notion of God's sovereignty over all places evoked in the text from Malachi, but retains the particular intramural focus on liturgical practice in the church. As such, the text is in keeping with the perspective of the direction for prayers on behalf of kings and authorities found in 1 Timothy 2.2.

The specific practice of prayer called for in 1 Timothy 2.8 envisions the lifting up of hands, designated specifically as 'holy hands'. Such an activity has Jewish liturgical precedent as evidenced in LXX texts (e.g. Ps. 27.2, 62.5, Lam. 2.19) and ancient carvings (e.g. the first-century BCE Rhenia Stele, 'a prayer of vengeance for two murdered women', in Deissmann, Fig. 75, 414-15). Quinn notes that early Christian references to the activity demonstrate a Christological origin in connecting the outstretched nature of the hands with the position of Christ on the cross. Such connections are made overtly by other early church Fathers (e.g. Justin and Tertullian), so it is difficult to discern if the PE letter writer intends such a reference. At the very least the early Jewish pietistic references to God's eternity, unity and sovereignty cited in previous doxological and confessional formulae (e.g. 1 Tim. 1.17 and 2.5-6) are dramatized here in the letter writer's description of the ideal male supplicant.

The description of the upraised hands as 'holy' further delineates the parameters of how men should pray in the community. For Paul the term *hagio* would be the likely choice for 'holy' with its cultic sense of sanctification for the purpose of approaching God. The letter writer's use of *hosio* bears a cultic meaning not within Israel's scriptural tradition, but the Greek mystery religions. The term is more religio-ethically focused on right behaviour than sanctification (BAGD, 589). This nuance comes into focus at the culmination of the letter writer's injunction that men do their praying apart from anger or dispute. The letter writer imagines division in the community about the practice of worship as tantamount to unholiness. For the letter writer the practice of peaceful prayer, and worship without dispute, is a means of tangibly acknowledging the church's confession of the sovereignty and unity of God.

Many interpreters have noted the disparate relationship between the treatment of men in 1 Timothy 2.8 and women in 1 Timothy 2.9-15 (e.g. Bassler, Schüssler Fiorenza, Schottroff). No doubt the letter writer provides more instruction for women, and the teachings have a broader application in the lives of women. Important, however, is what connects the treatment of the two groups. In both cases, the letter writer is concerned with restricting certain undesired elements of speech within the church. The men are called to pray without debate (*dialogismou*), while the women are called to learn in silence, in other words they are not to speak. Certainly the repressive treatment of women's speech exceeds that of men within this unit; however in both cases limitations are being placed on both groups and their practice of speaking. In this men and women alike are being ordered by the letter writer to accept a model of behaviour that comprises his ideal vision of the church.

Unlike the directions for men in 1 Timothy 2.8, the letter writer's directions for women in 1 Timothy 2.9-15 are not limited to the liturgical field. At the conclusion of the unit stands an interpretation of Genesis 2.4b-3.18 that grounds the writer's claims about women in their essential biology. The writer's appeal to and particular interpretation of Genesis 2-3 and his generalization of Eve's transgression to include all women transforms his directions from the particularities of specific church context to a global statement about the nature and limitations of all women. This dramatic shift to such a global statement about women on the basis of such a primary authority as Genesis underscores the gravity of the letter writer's concerns about the speech of certain women. Such women are not merely a sideline disturbance for the letter writer. Rather their presence and teaching in the community threatens to undermine the foundations of the letter writer's view of the church and society in general.

The directions regarding women in 1 Timothy 2.9-15 likely represent a diverse collection of teachings that were later assembled by the letter writer. 1 Timothy 2.9-10, following on 'likewise', takes up issues related to women's clothing, hairstyles, and general comportment. 1 Timothy 2.11-15 (3.1), however, begins with a new hortatory subjunctive in the phrase 'Let women learn in silence, in complete submission.' 1 Timothy 2.12, then, reintroduces the voice of the letter writer heard earlier in 1 Timothy 2.8 ('I desire') with the prohibition: 'I do not permit'. In both content and tone verses 11-12 are more strident than the claims regarding apparel in verses 9-10. Yet the letter writer has placed the two sections together as a series addressing both the specific issue of women's dress and the more general social issue of their role in relation to men.

The letter writer caps off these various claims about women with an exegetical rationale in 1 Timothy 2.13-15. The exegesis of Genesis 2.4-3.18 seems most connected to the second proscription. In other words, women are denied relationships of authority and leadership over men because of the cited interpretation of the Garden myth. According to the letter writer Adam (understood as 'man') was formed first and 'woman' second. Moreover women, as represented by Eve, were more prone to deception and transgression than men. Such foundational claims provide the basis for organizing men and women's roles in relation to one another. These are not merely transitory claims made to weather a particular storm of opponents or troublemakers in the church. Nor are they simply a pragmatic means to blend in with acceptable social practice in Hellenistic culture. These are essentialist claims, tied to a meta-narrative of God's original purposes for creation, extrapolated to speak forcefully to the letter writer's context, and understood to lay bare the truth of God's eternal sovereign design.

There is a marked disparity between the somewhat modest particulars of 1 Timothy's instructions and the far-reaching theological and hermenutical claims upon which they are based. In the case of 1 Timothy 2.8-15 (3.1), such disparity has led some commentators to suspect more than mere pragmatism in the demand that women submit to the authority of men. Luise Schottroff has described the rhetoric of 1 Timothy 2.8-15 as 'misogynistic'. It is an example not so much of accepted Greco-Roman social practice aimed at women's decorum in worship, as of the culture's unabashed hatred of women's freedom within everyday life, inclusive of worship (Schottroff, 70).

Such hatred was, according to Schottroff, a part of a larger Greco-Roman cultural movement directed at women who were resisting patriarchal oppression. Schottroff cites the historical example of the Oppian Laws of 215 BCE and their repeal in 195 BCE. These laws had served to restrict the amount of gold a woman could wear, subdue their choices in clothing and place restrictions on their travel into cities and towns, save for religious festivals. According to Mary Lefkowitz and Maureen B. Fant, the laws had their origin in Rome's defeat by Hannibal in 215 BCE (Lefkowitz and Fant, 177). They sought to stem a crisis of war shortages by curtailing women's consumption of luxury items (e.g. gold and expensive clothing). Once the war had passed, women sought the repeal of the laws. To this end, they were successful, but only for a time.

The Roman historian Tacitus provides a record of the debates over the laws that rings with echoes of the rhetoric of 1 Timothy 2.8-15. In the discussion of women, their weak nature, and their 'natural' place one can hear a hint of fear about women's potential power to transgress the status quo and threaten male privilege. In her interpretation of 1 Timothy 2 Schottroff cites the speech of Severus Caiecina in Tacitus, *Annals* 3.33-34:

> The female gender is weak and unable to deal with strain; when the reins are loosened, it is brutal, ambitious, and power hungry women enter the ranks of soldiers and make centurions do a handyman's work .... Once they are reined in by the Oppian Laws and other regulations; now, let loose, they give orders in private households, the law courts, and even the armed forces. (cited in Schottroff, 70)

Appeals to the weak nature of women and to the necessity of patriarchal control of the household are based in ancient tradition. In both the Oppian debates and the rhetoric of 1 Timothy it is clear that seemingly minor restrictions on women's dress and comportment have a deep and abiding connection to larger concerns regarding their economic, political and social power. The reins must not be loosened, and women must be silent. At once weak and very powerful, women must be strictly controlled by male authority. If not, the consequences are disorder, transgression and chaos.

Behind the rhetoric of the debates about the Oppian Laws and the argument of 1 Timothy 2.8-15 there stands an important, but as Schottroff notes, unwitting witness. These demands for women's submission can be read between the lines for a history of women's struggle against oppressive economic, social, political and ecclesial structures. In Livy's history the story is told that in their protest at the Oppian Laws the women of Rome in an organized protest took to the streets and blocked the entrance to the Forum over a period of days, finally winning the repeal of the laws for a time (cited in Lefkowitz and Fant, 177). These women who stubbornly stood in the Forum's entrance and won the laws' repeal challenge Severus Caiecina's claims about women's inherent lack of discipline, and their inability to function outside of male control. Just so, the demands of the writer of 1 Timothy that women are to learn in silence and submission seem to indicate that some women may actually have been speaking in the church with authority. Why would the letter writer bother to enjoin women to silence, unless they are already talking? Why would he command women's submission to male authority, unless a challenge had already been made to that structure? The rhetoric of 1 Timothy 2.8-15 belies the writer's construction of the 'ideal' vision of church life. The commands, the directions, and the exhortations are evidence of dispute, dissension and 'other ways' of being church.

Finally, the letter writer's demand for men to avoid disputes (*dialogia*) in 1 Timothy 2.8 indicates that such a controversy was not so much a battle of the sexes, as it was a dispute among churches about how their social lives and relationships should be ordered. Commanding men not to take part in disputes, therefore, is yet another unwitting witness by the letter writer to the fact that some men were in disagreement with the order that women be silent and not teach or have authority over men within the church.

An important witness to this other way of being church is found in the early Christian apocryphal work the *Acts of Paul*. As noted in the Introduction, a portion of this work tells the story of Thecla, a young woman of Iconium in Asia Minor, who was compelled by the preaching of Paul, and who spurned her expected social role in order to become an apostle. This story provides compelling evidence of the situation of women in the early church's varying interpretations of the writings of Paul.

In the story, Thecla hears Paul's call to abstain from marriage (based in 1 Cor. 7.8), and she rejects her betrothal to Thamyris in order to follow Paul and pursue the life of an apostle. This enrages Thamyris, Thecla's mother, Theocleia, and the servants in Thecla's household. Thecla's bold initiative to respond to Paul's teaching, and to abandon her expected roles as wife, daughter and female member of her household upsets the entire order of her community.

Dennis MacDonald in his work, *The Legend and the Apostle: The Battle for Paul in Story and Canon*, imagines the opponents of the Pastoral Epistle writer to be informed by the legendary apostolic authority of women figures such as Thecla. MacDonald demonstrates uncanny rhetorical parallels between the characterization of opponents in the PE and the description of Paul by Theocleia in the *Acts of Paul*. For example:

> 2 Timothy 3.6-7
> For among them are those who make their ways into households and capture weak women burdened by sins and swayed by various impulses, who will listen to anybody and can never arrive at any knowledge of the truth.
>   Thamyris, this man [Paul] is upsetting the city of the Iconians, and thy Thecla in addition; for all the women and young people go to him

and are taught by him. 'You must,' he says, 'fear one single god, and
live chastely.' And my daughter also, who sticks to the window like a
spider, is moved by his words and gripped by new desire ... for the
maiden hangs upon the things he says, and is taken captive.
(Schneemelcher, *New Testament Apocrypha*, vol. 2, p. 240)

As MacDonald's work makes clear, the story of Thecla and the PE
witness to a broad argument within the early church over the
interpretation of Paul. Clearly Paul's instructions regarding sexual
abstinence in 1 Corinthians 7.8 were read by some early Christians as a
charter for a social order in which women were no longer tied to the
patriarchal household as wives and servants. Other Christians, such as
the Pastoral Epistle writer, did not interpret Paul in this way. In both of
these different communities Paul's writings were authoritative. It was
their interpretation of Paul that varied.

This dispute over the interpretation of Paul provides an important
hermeneutical lens for the demands for women's silence, submission
and absence from civil and church leadership in 1 Timothy 2.8-15. In
its proscriptions and claims the text bears witness to an atmosphere of
debate on these matters. Rather than accept the text as abiding
doctrine, or dismiss it as an antiquated relic, this perspective provides
the possibility of seeing the text as a window to view a holy argument
about the nature of Christian community. In addition, the text can
become less a window on history and more a mirror to reflect practices
of rhetoric and appeals to tradition in contemporary struggles for
women's equality. Far from a model of orthodoxy, 1 Timothy 2.8-15
provides insight into how ecclesial structures of domination were and
are formed. They are not 'natural' or 'inevitable', but rather they are
acts of power in a struggle over the interpretation of tradition. The
history of this contentious interpretation and its diverse social settings
continue to witness to the life of the church today.

The final appeal to tradition in 1 Timothy 2.14-15 is best understood
as an example of just such a rhetorical manoeuvre of power. Schottroff
demonstrates that such appeals to the original state of women's
subordinate status to men were not the sole domain of biblical
exegetes (Schottroff, 76). Similar claims were made regarding the
station of women within pagan literature. In both cases, the tradition
provided the basis for authorizing women's inferior status, and
lamenting the current state of affairs. Likewise, the tradition continues
to provide an appeal to 'the good old days' as leverage to disparage the
current quest for women's freedom. Lefkowitz and Fant provide an
example of Roman rhetorician Marcus Porcius Cato appealing to
ancestral authority regarding women in Livy's *History of Rome* 34.1-8:

> Our ancestors did not want women to conduct any, not even private, business without a guardian. They wanted them to be under the authority of parents, brothers, or husbands; we (the gods help us!) even now let them snatch at the government and meddle in the Forum and our assemblies. (Lefkowitz and Fant, 177)

In 1 Timothy 2.14-15 the letter writer employs the ancient tradition of Genesis 2.3 in order to support his claims about women. His argument for women's submission to male authority is based upon an exegetical insight about temporal relationship in the text between the creation of Adam and the creation of Eve. This argument using temporal priority to explain relational superiority has precedent in other early Jewish and Christian exegesis. Paul himself uses the technique of temporal priority, though perhaps more creatively, in Romans 4.9-12 where he argues that faith was reckoned to Abraham as righteousness prior to his taking on circumcision. Specifically, Paul notes that Abraham had faith (LXX *pistis*) and that the Lord reckoned it to him as righteousness (LXX *dikaisoune*) in Genesis 15.6 prior to his circumcision in Genesis 17.24. From this observation Paul then deduces that faith has priority to circumcision. Circumcision, in other words, is not a prerequisite for faith. The reasoning behind this type of exegetical technique is that what happens first is more important than that which happens subsequently. Similarly in his determination that the ostensible temporal precedence of Adam's creation to that of Eve's in Genesis 2 signifies Adam's superiority, the PE writer is acting very much within an exegetical convention of his time.

Feminist Hebrew Bible scholar Phyllis Trible has challenged the interpretation of the priority of Adam's creation in Genesis 2-3. In her work *God and the Rhetoric of Sexuality* she carefully scrutinizes the terms for male and female in relation to the event of human creation. Trible notes that contrary to interpretations which follow in the path of 1 Timothy 2.13-14 'woman' was not created after 'man'. Indeed in Genesis 2.6-7 when God creates the human being that figure is an ungendered, undifferentiated creature of mud (*adamah*). According to Trible this is the creation of a human, but not the creation of a sexually differentiated human. The differentiation between the sexes comes in the division of the *adamah* into man (*ish*) and woman (*ishah*) in Genesis 2.21-22. In this interpretation there is no temporal priority to the creation of males. In fact, both men and women are created from the 'mud creature' simultaneously at the time that God divides the creature at the rib. Such an interpretation, attentive to the technical language for gender in the text, resists the notion of temporal superiority in the creation of males.

In 1 Timothy 2.14 the letter writer provides a second scriptural basis beyond mere temporal inferiority to bolster his claims against women's authority in relation to men. He moves from simply stating a hierarchical relationship of men over women, to enumerating the original and inherent flaw of woman's character. Moving to Genesis 3.1-18, the writer notes that within the primordial drama of the Garden of Eden 'woman' (exemplified by Eve) was deceived (by the serpent) and became the transgressor.

The particular character of the letter writer's appropriation of Genesis 3.13 can be appreciated further by examining Paul's own use of the text. In 2 Corinthians 11.3 Paul appeals to Eve's having been deceived by the serpent in clear reference to the tradition of Genesis 3.1-18. Paul, however, does not apply that event to an assessment of the original design of women. Rather he connects Eve's transgression to the propensity of all people (men and women) to be deceived. In 2 Corinthians, Paul is concerned with speech that transgresses his authority, much as the writer of 1 Timothy. However, the speech is that of any person in the community who does not adhere to Paul's gospel, and the transgression is not of male authority in general, but Paul's authority as an apostle in particular. The rhetorical and exegetical particularities of 1 Timothy 2.13-15 provide insight into a context in which authority has become generalized from Paul's particular example and person into a larger structure of male domination and hierarchical control understood as the 'church'. Such an appropriation of tradition demonstrates a development beyond Paul, and reveals a context of discord about the issue of women and authority within and without the letter writer's community.

While the letter writer's exegesis demonstrates a particularly innovative and androcentrically chauvinistic interpretation of Genesis 3, it also reveals the prevailing concern of 1 Timothy as a whole. On the face of things the writer appears to be concerned with establishing a rigid social order of men over women. His greater anxiety, however, is with transgression and subversive speech from both men and women. In other words, the letter writer's most pressing concern is to assert and maintain right belief (as opposed to 'other teachings') in his community. However, women, as corroborated by the writer's concern regarding the speech of unattached women (widows) in 1 Timothy 5.13, pose a specific threat of transgressive, heretical speech. For this reason, their position in the community must be, according to the writer, carefully ordered and controlled.

The letter writer's interpretation of Genesis 2-3 is entirely driven by his need to establish his singular definition of authority within the church. It has already been noted that in addition to the repression of women's speech and authority evident in 1 Timothy 2.11-12 the letter writer commands the men of the church to pray without anger or disagreement, literally 'dialogue' (*dialogismou*). Just as women are commanded to silence, men are commanded not to argue. It seems that with regard to speech that subverts his authority and teaching the letter writer is gender blind. He commands obedience from men and women alike. By taking into consideration his central concern regarding transgressive speech, and by not focusing on his binary gender divisions so often examined by interpreters, the letter writer comes off as no less misogynistic, but the oppressive character of his vision of the church can be seen to apply to both men and women.

As with the interpretation of the temporal relationship between Adam and Eve's creation, more recent exegetes have challenged the notion that Eve is necessarily the one to blame for the transgression in the Garden of Eden. Danna Nolan Fewell and David Gunn in their work *Gender, Power, and Promise: The Subject of the Bible's First Story* use a feminist narrative critical approach to read and trouble the text of Genesis 2-3 and its traditional interpretation. In their essay on the creation story entitled 'Shifting the Blame' they demonstrate that a close reading of the Genesis text reveals troubling tensions in the presentation of all the characters, including God in the story. Fewell and Gunn ask the question of why Eve has been traditionally blamed for taking the fruit, and why interpreters have been reluctant to engage the more troubling question of why God placed the forbidden tree in the garden in the first place. In this regard, Fewell and Gunn empathize with Eve, and understand her taking of the fruit to be a courageous and bold step, rather than a transgression. She desires the fruit precisely because as one created by God she aspires toward God's presence:

> the woman's adventurous spirit, analogous to God's need for discovery, exhibits courage. She is willing to take risks. She is comfortable with lack of closure. She does not know what is going to happen. Obviously neither does God. (Fewell and Gunn, 31)

In many ways the favourable interpretation of Eve's actions in Genesis 3 by Fewell and Gunn echoes an early feminist interpreter of the text in the late nineteenth century. In *The Woman's Bible*, published in 1898 to serve the cause of women's suffrage, Elizabeth Cady Stanton and her colleagues set out to critique the androcentric and patriarchal tone of scripture. They both re-imagined the meaning of certain texts and called for the canonical removal of others as they battled with

Protestant clergymen who sought to thwart the right of women to vote with proof texts selected from scripture. In their reinterpretation of Genesis 2-3 *The Woman's Bible* commentators, and Stanton in particular, noted that a close reading of the text evoked much more sympathy on behalf of Eve than Adam.

> In this prolonged interview, the unprejudiced reader must be impressed with the courage, the dignity, and the lofty ambitions of the woman. The tempter evidently had a profound knowledge of human nature, and saw at a glance the high character of the person he met by chance in his walks in the garden. He did not try to tempt her from the path of duty by brilliant jewels, rich dresses, worldly luxuries or pleasures, but with knowledge, and the wisdom of the Gods. Like Socrates or Plato, his powers of conversation and asking puzzling questions, were no doubt marvelous, and he roused in the woman that intense thirst for knowledge, that the simple pleasures of picking flowers and talking with Adam did not satisfy. Compared with Adam she appears to great advantage through the entire story. (Stanton, *et al.*, 24-25).

The letter writer's final directions about women shift from the imperative to the declarative mood. 1 Timothy 2.15 appears to draw on tradition from Genesis 3.16 in which the lot of women is described as frequent and painful childbirth. Here the letter writer expands this notion to that of salvation. Quinn and Wacker see a citation of a liturgical formula in this case, from a marriage ceremony that drew upon the Genesis tradition to establish the roles of men and women, and to promote the purpose of the union in procreation. In this case, the reference to an established liturgical formula would provide a personal connection for many of the letter writer's addressees who may remember hearing this formula recited at their own marriage ceremonies. Evoking this formula grounds the letter writer's claims in a common experience within the community, and to a set of promises, and thereby to another authority, already acknowledged by the women and men of the community. Importantly, this assent has occurred within the structure of the patriarchal household, providing the letter writer yet another example of the divine authority of that structure.

In examining the notion of sexuality and gender present in 1 Timothy 2.13-15 it is difficult to assess how the church had come to this interpretation of Paul. In 1 Corinthians 7.8ff., for example, Paul calls the Corinthian Christians, men and women, to remain as he is, in other words, to be celibate. In this direction Paul informs his community that men and women have a place of value within the life of the church outside of the patriarchal household. Remarkably for

Paul the sexuality of women within marriage is seen as having the potential to 'consecrate' and thereby 'save' their heathen husbands (1 Corinthians 7.13-16). In Paul's understanding women may choose to be celibate within the church or they may use their bodies and sexuality within marriage to affect God's plan of redemption and salvation in the world.

The Pastoral Epistle writer's engagement of sexuality and gender redirects the teaching of Paul in 1 Corinthians 7 in a manner that might be described as a 'backlash'. In the name of Paul the letter writer teaches his community that in order to have a place of any value within the church, in order to be 'saved', women must participate within the structure of the patriarchal household. Women are to bear children and to conduct themselves in faith, love and holiness (*hagiasmo*). Remarkably this notion of women's holiness is completely stripped of its agency and power in 1 Corinthians 7.14 where Paul had argued that women – and men – have the potential in marriage to make holy (*hagiastai*) their unbelieving spouses. It is clear that Paul believes that sexual intercourse is the vehicle of this consecration and that the children of this union according to Paul are holy (*hagia*). Procreative activity within marriage between at least one believing person and another is a means to production of holiness. In a reversal of Paul's understanding of the positive function of women's sexual agency the writer of 1 Timothy establishes, in Paul's name, an understanding of women as dangerously transgressive and transforms their role in sanctification from one of agent to one of recipient. Consequently, the letter writer of 1 Timothy constructs for women a social reality in the church that is in direct contradiction to the teachings of Paul found in Paul's uncontested letters.

The idea that women are to receive salvation (*sothesetai*) through childbearing is a remarkable claim. Whether this idea is borne out of the liturgical traditions (as Quinn and Wacker assert) or is the letter writer's own construction, it reveals the objectification of women's bodies and their vocational purposes into the direct service of the patriarchal household. Margaret Atwood in her haunting futuristic novel *The Handmaid's Tale* depicts a world (the Republic of Gilead) in which certain women are enslaved into households for the sheer purpose of procreation. They are treated as concubines and raped for the purpose of impregnation. The viability of their lives is directly related to the viability of their ovaries and their uteruses to produce children for the household. These women are the Handmaids, and they are prohibited to be literate, to have community with one another or to any self-agency. While Atwood's novel is clearly part satire, part moral tale, part prophetic warning, her creation of Gilead and the handmaid system seems to illustrate the components of a world which is grounded in the notion that women's salvation comes through their ability to produce children – where women are reduced in their identity to the material production of their bodies. Such a world necessitates rigid control over women's bodies and the systematic and often violent division of women's agency and sense of self from their bodies. Atwood's novel seems to provide a vivid narrative description of the kind of world that the PE letter writer holds forth as the ideal church in 1 Timothy 2.8-15.

In a similar artistic endeavour playwright Eve Ensler dramatically presents the variety of interviews she conducted with women about the subject of their vaginas. In this piece entitled *The Vagina Monologues,* which has been translated into twenty-two languages and performed throughout the world, Ensler seeks to challenge the kind of objectification of women and their genitals detailed in 1 Timothy 2.15 and presents an alternative notion of women's salvation to be whole selves through the reclaiming and full experience of their vaginas. In Ensler's vision 'salvation' comes to women through their vaginas, but does so through a woman's experience of the joy, pleasure, pain and purpose of what it means to be a woman. In her vision women's lives and bodies are not designed by God to serve the production of children for the patriarchal household, but rather women live toward the end of being women, of bringing life through childbirth, yes, but also in myriad other ways through sexual pleasure, love, anger, the struggle for social justice and seeking the greater good for all humankind.

As a contemporary feminist interpreter of 1 Timothy 2.8-15 I am delighted by the ironic turn of events that today a woman by the name of Eve has used her voice to provide a dramatic forum within which women are called to salvation through the reclaiming of their own vaginas. While Ensler is not directly responding to the PE writer in her dramatic series of monologues about women and their vaginas, it is clear that her insights and her project to give voice to women and their sexual power stand in opposition to the PE letter writer's understanding of women and their purpose in divine creation.

In reading 1 Timothy 2.8-15 one might wonder what the letter writer's directions about women would have sounded like to a woman outside the legitimacy of the patriarchal household. What may his claims about childbearing and salvation have meant to women who were infertile or unattached to men, either through death or lack of marriage? The fact that such contingencies are not addressed demonstrates that the letter writer is not directly concerned with such women in his community. Rather than caring for the individuals of the church, it seems, the letter writer is establishing the legitimacy of masculine authority in the church, and as such addresses men about the 'ideal' arrangement of women's roles in the community. Particular women and their particular situations outside of this ideal are not his concern in the letter. In this sense, I have always wondered about the designation of 1 Timothy as a 'Pastoral Epistle'. Indeed, its tone and focus on the structure of the church over and above personal concerns seems the opposite of what I have come to understand as a 'pastoral' sensibility. If 1 Timothy reflects issues of pastoral concern, how are the women of the community cared for in his teachings? Recently some students of mine in the seminar 'Following Paul', about the late first and early second-century interpretation of the Apostle, came to refer to the PE as the 'Un-pastoral Epistles'.

The writer's directions about men and women conclude with the formulaic phrase 'the saying is sure', in 1 Timothy 3.1. Quinn and Wacker argue that this phrase refers to the liturgical formula cited in 1 Timothy 2.15. Whatever the role of this little fragment, it does serve to underscore the entire unit's concern with right speech in the church. Men are to pray without argument, women, due to their inherent propensity to deception and transgression, are to be silent and submit to male authority. Speech, right speech, is the central concern of the letter writer throughout the unit. This final declaration of 'the saying is sure' produces a model of the church and its traditions (both biblical and liturgical) that is seen to be trustworthy and authoritative. While anxiety about transgressive speech and 'other teachings' bleed through the cracks of the writer's assertions and directions, he busily constructs his ideal church on the foundation of claims to soundness and certainty.

1 Timothy 3.1-7 and 1 Timothy 3.8-13: Bishops and deacons as ideal men

In 1 Timothy 3.1-13 the letter writer turns his attention to ecclesial offices. He outlines the comportment and qualifications of bishops (3.1-7) and deacons (3.8-13). Implicitly, the unit presupposes the social order described in 1 Timothy 2.8-15 because these offices are delineated as for men only (i.e. 1 Tim. 3.2: 'the bishop must be the husband of one wife', and 1 Timothy 3.12: 'the deacon is to be the husband of one wife'). These expectations are coordinated with the requirement that such men will manage their own households and children well. As the letter writer has interpreted Genesis 2-3 to provide God's original design of male authority over women in 1 Timothy 2.13-15, he here implies the presence of that same design in the church. Bishops and deacons are expected to sustain hierarchical male power in both their ecclesial and personal lives.

The division of these realms, church and household, sheds some light on the letter writer's distance from the undisputed letters of Paul. Paul has no household, and he manages no family. Paul manages churches and members of those churches manage their own households, but he himself does not head a household. The letter writer provides an image of the church for the gaze of the state and broader culture. Church leaders are understood to have both professional and private lives. Moreover there is an assumption that they have a public persona while performing their duties and responsibilities. Bishops must be seen well by those from outside (1 Tim. 3.6), and deacons are to aspire to good standing for themselves. Such efforts provide fortification for the church against slanderous forces, and uncertainty in the faith.

The term 'bishop' (*episkopos*) literally means 'one who oversees', or 'overseer'. In Greek non-biblical sources the term has many uses. At times it is connected with cultic settings, but more generally it designates the supervision of matters of the state and education (Liddell and Scott, 552). In early Jewish sources the term is tied to the task of oversight; it is not an established, particular kind of office. For example, in Philippians 1.1 Paul greets the bishops (plural) and deacons (also plural) as a special designation in his address to the saints in Christ Jesus who are in Philippi. Paul, however, does not designate the activities of these persons, nor does he indicate their order or rank in the church. Ostensibly there were several bishops in the church at Philippi.

In 1 Timothy 3.1-7 the letter writer describes the position of bishop as an official position in the church to which one can aspire. The wish to be bishop (a single bishop) is the wish to do good, important work. The designation of the activity of bishop as work (*ergos*) is itself significant. This is an office, which is consistent with other named offices in the letter (e.g. *presbuterosin*, 1 Tim. 5.17ff.). The office of bishop bears particular responsibilities and practices. As is clear elsewhere in the letter, those who hold offices are regularly financially compensated (e.g. 1 Tim. 5.17).

Just as the notion of office seems to bespeak responsibilities, it is important to note that the description of the bishop in 1 Timothy 3.1-7 pertains not so much to the bishop's actual duties as to his comportment as a man. The same is true for what follows in

1 Timothy 3.8ff. regarding deacons. For the bishop, the list of dos and don'ts is headed by the phrase, *anepilemton*, 'beyond reproach'. The term occurs two other times in 1 Timothy 5.17 and 6.14 with regard to the behaviour of widows and in a closing charge to Timothy to keep the teachings unstained and beyond reproach. The particular charges that follow fall under this more general posture. Being the husband of one wife, temperate, sensible, hospitable, a skilled teacher, not a drunk, not violent, not argumentative, not greedy, are all a part of being 'beyond reproach'. Reproach is the central concern and entails a posture of being watched. Such a careful construction of the bishop's protocol makes it clear that in order to be effective at the work of oversight the one who is charged with this work must be spotless in the sight of all.

Many commentators note that the list for bishops, like the list for deacons in 1 Timothy 3.8-13, represents a stock Hellenistic catalogue of attributes for the moral life. These virtues make up, in other words, the qualities of the ideal man. In this sense, the letter writer is not here giving a list of actual qualifications, as in a check list, for these officials, but rather he is communicating that church leaders are to be of the highest moral character.

In both 1 Timothy 3.1-7 and 3.8-13, the writer provides a clue to the practical purpose for the irreproachable character of bishops and deacons. High officials are subject, he notes, to traps (*pagida*, 1 Tim. 3.7), and their visibility can either build or erode confidence in the faith that is in Christ Jesus (1 Tim. 3.13). In this sense, bishops and deacons make the church strong through their high moral example; their public example can be a means through which to attract more people to the confession of faith.

Raymond Collins in his commentary on 1 and 2 Timothy and Titus notes that the list of qualifications for deacons in 1 Timothy 3.8-13 bears five qualities that are necessary for the position. These qualities according to Collins are stock virtues in Hellenistic catalogues. Polycarp in his letter to the Philippians lists the same qualities (*Pol.* 4.3). One deacon requirement which the PE writer and Polycarp share that is not found in traditional lists of virtues is the notion of 'not being double tongued' (*me dilogous*), (Collins, 89). In this sense the PE writer and Polycarp share a peculiar preoccupation with speech that is not divided, but rather conforms with the letter writer's understanding of authority and truth. Such a preoccupation is endemic to their struggle of battling 'other teachings' that also find authority and truth in the writings of Paul, but render different interpretations from those writings. Such a shared concerned with 'divided speech' underscores their common anxiety about the power of authoritative teachings to both direct and confound their churches. Disputes, disagreement and double-tongued speech underlie their desire to establish and proclaim the unitary nature of Paul's teaching and the leadership of the church.

In the midst of the letter writer's carefully prescribed lists of conduct for bishops and deacons stands a challenging and perhaps anomalous verse. In 1 Timothy 3.11 the list of deacon prescriptions is interrupted by the phrase 'Women likewise must be serious, not slanderers, but temperate and faithful in all things.' The central question in interpreting this interruption is: are these 'women' a parallel group of women deacons, or are they the 'wives' of the already-mentioned deacons?

In early Christian literature there is ample evidence that women served in the church as deacons. For example, Paul commends Phoebe whom he names as a 'deacon' in the church of Cenchreae, to the Roman Christians (Rom. 16.1). By examining early strata of the gospel traditions, scholars have detected evidence that women may have served much as 'the Twelve' in the Jesus movement. In Mark 15.40-41 Mary Magdalene, Mary the mother of James the younger and Joses, and Salome are named among those women who when Jesus was in Galilee 'followed him, and ministered to him (*diakoneo*)'. These are verbs that are ascribed to the official Twelve male disciples within the gospels. In addition the verb *diakoneo* is associated in early Christian literature with the activities of those designated as 'table servers', or deacons in the church.

The question for 1 Timothy 3.11, therefore, is not whether women may have been deacons in the life of the early church in general. We already know that they served in such a capacity. The question is whether women in the PE writer's church were allowed such positions of leadership. In light of the assessment of women's social role in 1 Timothy 2.11-12 and the further draconian delineation of their place within salvation history as 'transgressor' (1 Tim. 2.14) it is difficult to imagine that the letter writer would then so casually in 1 Timothy 3.11 describe their work in the community among the elite leadership of bishops and deacons. Rather, the verse may be a portion of an older catalogue in the church on expectations for women who held the office of deacon, which the letter writer clumsily attempted to incorporate into his letter. Or perhaps more likely, since the Greek term *gune* can be translated as 'woman' or 'wife', 1 Timothy 3.11 refers to the wives of deacons who like their husbands were expected to behave decorously and suitably within church and society. Indeed, like bishops in 1 Timothy 3.2, deacons are required in 1 Timothy 3.12 to be 'the husband of one wife'. It seems that this requirement alone within the letter writer's understanding of the social organization of the church would disqualify women for the job.

While the central issue for the letter writer in 1 Timothy 2.8-15 is right speech, the concern in chapter 3 is focused on right appearance. On the one hand the letter writer understands that right speech keeps the church pure and trustworthy before God, on the other hand the correct appearance of its leaders keeps it strong within the sight of the world. For the letter writer the two concerns are the Scylla and Charybdis through which he steers his church. Purity of belief and practice protected the church as the 'pillar and bulwark of truth' (1 Timothy 3.15), but respectability within the sight of the larger community and world offered the church a position within which to appear strong and undivided. Women, children and slaves within the letter writer's understanding were the household members who were expected to cooperate for the sake of the smoothly functioning church. Their lives, though disregarded in many ways, were the necessary element for the properly functioning church and household. Attending to their presence and their voices between the lines of 1 Timothy is a means of both honouring their struggle against their objectification, and demanding that throughout the world and in the church people of similar plights are not ignored, and the cause of the struggle for their freedom is taken up.

1 Timothy 3.14-4.16:
Fighting the Opponents

Introduction

This central unit of 1 Timothy is the least well-defined of any of the portions of the letter and yet its verses contain sentiments that seem most fully to capture the purpose of the entire correspondence. The unit is one of the few places in the letter where the writer seems to directly address the recipient(s) and thereby provides the opportunity for the writer to underscore what he hopes the letter will achieve and what he hopes the recipient(s) will do. The unit contains: 1. mention of Paul's situation of travel and the occasion for sending the instructions (1 Timothy 3.14-16); 2. some description of the practices of those whom the letter writer has defined as having 'departed from the faith' (4.1-4); and 3. instructions for 'Timothy' to behave as a 'good minister' of Jesus Christ and to teach and instruct the brethren until Paul should return to Ephesus. In a sense the unit stands as an epistolary intermission between the ecclesial rules regarding bishops and deacons in 1 Timothy 3.1-13 and the expectations for behaviour of widows, elders and slaves in 1 Timothy 5.1-6.2.

One recurring rhetorical element does bind this loosely defined unit together. In 1 Timothy 3.14, 4.6, 4.11 and 4.14 the letter writer uses the near demonstrative pronoun substantively in the neuter plural to denote 'these things' (*tauta*). Repeatedly, throughout the unit, the letter writer directs the recipient(s) to heed, teach and command 'these things'. He seems to be refering to those elements about worship, women's behaviour, bishops and deacons that he has already discussed in 1 Timothy 1.1-3.13, and to those elements regarding widows, elders and slaves which he will provide in 1 Timothy 5.1-6.2. In a sense, this reprieve from the content of ecclesiastical rules found in the earlier and following units demonstrates the fragmentary nature of the letter.

Already in the discussion of 1 Timothy 3.8-13 it became clear that the letter writer uses pre-assembled lists of rules and duties to present the content of his teaching to the recipient(s). The repeated use of the substantive neuter pronoun ('these things') may indicate that he understands himself to be passing on the general content of the church's teaching. 'These things' are not the writer's 'things'. They are not his particular revelation or wisdom. 'These things' are the church's things. The letter writer is in a position to pass on 'these things' about the church, and stands as one who encourages 'Timothy' to pass on 'these things' faithfully. As such the letter writer and Timothy are merely servants of the larger structure of the church. This central unit offers the writer an opportunity to step back from relaying the content of 'these things' and to challenge the recipient(s) to carry out their work faithfully in representing the instructions of the letter. It is a reminder of the letter writer's ('Paul's') role in passing along the correct teaching of the church to those who follow in his stead ('Timothy'). 'These things' do not change. Apparently what changes are the circumstances in which they are preached and taught, and the names of those who are called to preach and teach. 'These things' are the reliable words of the tradition that in the letter writer's understanding hold up the 'household of God, the pillar and bulwark of the truth' (1 Timothy 3.15).

1 Timothy 3.14-16a: Travel details and the purposes of the letter

After the lists of qualifications for bishops and deacons in 1 Timothy 3.1-13 the letter turns somewhat abruptly to more private communication between the letter writer and the recipients. This unevenness in the character of the letter, moving between formal ecclesial elements and more personal communication, has led some critics to assess its nature as quite fragmentary. From this perspective scholars understand that the letter writer has edited pieces of ecclesial directives and traditions together, and has interspersed into these more formal elements his own rhetorical construction of private correspondence in order to mimic the letter form. By this pseudepigraphical construction the letter writer hoped that these documents would attain the stature of long lost letters of Paul that had been suddenly and providentially found.

Importantly, areas of the letter that are constructed as private communication bear more than the mere formal pleasantries of greetings, thanksgivings and the like. In these areas (such as 1 Timothy 3.14-15) the letter writer shares content that tends to focus on his opponents and their activities. In spite of the ruse of the pseudepigraphical voice of Paul these units of private correspondence in 1 Timothy are important places to hear the voice and concerns of the letter writer. In contrast to the quoting and inserting of traditional material throughout much of the letter, the elements of personal and direct communication between 'Paul' and 'Timothy' most clearly bear the marks of the context of the church and the letter writer's struggles in that context. It is somewhat ironic that when the letter writer most intentionally poses as 'Paul', one who travelled and wrote letters to his churches, the contrivances of his practice of pseudepigraphy are most apparent. Such moments in 1 Timothy provide the opportunity to peel back the letter writer's mask and sneak a peek at his underlying concerns.

In the unit of 1 Timothy 3.14-16a the letter writer engages in second-person, direct address, and refers to the personal situation of 'Paul'. This rhetorical move is effective within the practice of pseudepigraphy as it reminds the readers/hearers of Paul's itinerant ministry which had been made legendary by the late first century by his widely circulated letters, the Acts of the Apostles and apocryphal non-canonical texts, such as the *Acts of Paul*. As depicted in these documents, Paul's work was often interrupted by various crises and contingencies of travel. In his own letters Paul signs off with reference to travel, as was a general custom within Greco-Roman letter writing (e.g. 1 Cor. 16.5-7). By evoking this style, the letter writer attempts to hook his readers/hearers back to the 'real' Paul. In addition he reminds the audience of Paul's absence to underscore the importance of this teaching, and the authority of these instructions for the proper administration of the church.

Throughout the opening and closing sections of his uncontested letters Paul refers to his travel among his churches. In places his travel is delayed by unforeseen circumstances (e.g. 1 Thes. 2.17-19), and in other places he changes his plans according to what is best in his ministry (e.g. 2 Cor. 1.12-24). For Paul travel and its attendant delays was an integral part of his work. In fact the letter and the use of emissaries (like Timothy, e.g. 1 Thes. 3.1-10) were extensions of Paul's limited capacity to be physically present with his churches. They were ways in which he extended himself, often with great anguish, to be present in some form with his churches.

In 1 Timothy 3.15 the letter writer evokes the motif of the travel delay in a rhetorically poignant and powerful way. The conditional 'if I am delayed . . .' leaves the reader of the letter hanging with a sense of great moment in reading these instructions. Of course Paul was delayed! After the writing of this letter Paul and Timothy likely never saw one another again, and these teachings have been delayed by several generations. Through the artifice of the false letter the writer is able to offer these instructions to the church as though they were Paul's parting or lost instructions to Timothy, his most intimate companion. In this clever construction, the letter lives to offer the writer's community his version of Paul's vision for the church. In this

way he harnesses the full authority of the legendary apostle to guide
and instruct his community about how to be the church. Moreover, he
taps into the anxiety created by Paul's absence and through these new-
found instructions he offers the church great solace. The letter is tailor-
made for the purposes of the fledgling leaders of this community. 'Paul'
was offering instructions for the life of the church, and it just so
happens that such were exactly what the letter writer's constituency in
the church needed. No doubt, they would be on the edge of their seats
expectantly listening for the next piece of providential wisdom.

In 1 Timothy 3.15 the writer describes the letter's ultimate purpose.
He writes these instructions so that the leaders of the church might
know 'how one ought to behave in the household of God'. The verse
discloses the letter's aim, right instruction and the writer's understanding of the church, 'the household of the living God, the pillar and
bulwark of truth'. The verb *anastrepho*, found here in the passive
voice in conjunction with the verb *dei*, evokes the notion of behaviour
or conduct. The noun of this word-family (*anastrophe*) appears in this
same section in 1 Timothy 4.12 where the letter writer commands
'Timothy' to 'behave' in an exemplary way. In this sense, the letter's
ultimate purpose seems to be to provide instruction for and to
command 'appropriate behaviour' for all who are in the church,
leaders and members alike.

The image of the church as the 'household' (*oikos*) of God recalls
the fervent expectations of the letter writer for the behaviour of
bishops (1 Tim. 3.3, 5) and deacons (1 Tim. 3.12) in relation to their
own private households. Appropriate behaviour in the household of
God mirrors the order and paternal authority demanded of bishops and
deacons over their private households. In her feminist theological
reconstruction of Christian origins Elisabeth Schüssler Fiorenza notes
the effect of this overlap of expectations for male church leaders in
their private households and the 'household' of the church. Such a
confounding of the church's structure with the Greco-Roman social
order centralizes power within the hands of elite men and marginalizes
the power of women and slaves.

> The patriarchal order of the house, when applied to the order of the
> church, restricts the leadership of wealthy women and maintains
> social exploitation of slave-women and men, even within the
> Christian household community. (Schüssler Fiorenza, 291)

The letter writer's portrayal of 'Paul' instructing 'Timothy' about 'right
behaviour' presses the contrivance of the pseudepigraphical form. It is
hard to imagine that at the end of their long friendship and collegial

relationship Timothy would require such a formal treatise from Paul on 'right behaviour'. Here we can glimpse the way in which the letter writer projects the image and legend of Paul to reach out beyond personal correspondence to Timothy and toward the teaching of the whole community. In this sense the instructions do not resonate with those particular or personal directives found in Paul's uncontested letters. For example when Paul addresses two women personally in Philippians 4.2 he does not encourage their appropriate behaviour in a general way. Rather he calls them to 'have the same mind' in the Lord, which repeats his more general teaching of Philippians 2.5. In other words, Paul directly charges the women to agree and not to be in dispute with one another. In this letter Paul calls for 'correct behaviour' and does so in terms of his larger Christological teaching (Philippians 2.5-11), but he connects it with and responds to their particular situation, and does not seek to lay down a general command for 'correct behaviour'. In the posture of 'overhearing' the instructions of 1 Timothy, on the other hand, the recipients of the letter are provided with general instruction that they must apply to the particulars of their lives. In this sense the letter writer seems to seek to minimize the problematic particularity of Paul's letters, while maximizing the general authority of Paul's words and example to direct the behaviour of his church.

In addition to its reach outside of the relationship between Paul and Timothy, the term 'right behaviour' indicates the special emphasis of the letter writer's concern. The appearance of the church, both in its leadership and membership, is extremely important to the letter writer. In this sense he is not correcting the beliefs of those in the church as much he is correcting their practices. As such, it is clear that the intended audience of the letter is a group of insiders within the church who would already know the confessions of the church, but needed guidance regarding the pitfalls of improper practice. In calling attention to their practice of belief within the church the letter writer reminds them that only a small difference separates true faith from 'other teachings'. Plus, he is reminding them that he is watching their behaviour as the leaders of the church, and expecting their obedient conformity to his instructions. The call for 'correct behaviour' is a call that issues seamlessly from the posture of one who understands himself as *episkopos* - 'overseer' of the church.

In a sense, concern for 'correct behaviour' is still what guides the leadership of the church in its various expressions today. In the life of my own denomination, the Presbyterian Church (USA), oversight for the behaviour of clergy occupies a great deal of the energy of local presbytery leadership and committees. Clergy misconduct, particularly in areas of sexual and financial issues, sets the agenda for many meetings of the Committee on Ministry of various Presbyteries, which in many ways functions in PCUSA polity as the local 'Bishop'. It seems that the oversight of such issues of conduct among the leadership is an ongoing reality and burden for the institutional church.

The letter writer's emphasis on practice also reveals the central preoccupations of the orthodox thinking emerging from the late first and early second-century church. The practices of Christians divided them more than the language of their tradition and doctrine. As we see in the work of Elaine Pagels's *The Gnostic Paul* for example, the Gnostics were devout interpreters of the letters of Paul. An illustration of the Gnostic interpretations of Paul's letters can be seen in Pagels's detailing of the Valentinian interpretation of the resurrection of the dead in 1 Corinthians 15.12:

> What does Paul mean when he speaks of the 'resurrection of the dead'? The other apostles clearly proclaim this as the future, bodily resurrection of those who have died. But the Gnostic initiate rejects this preaching as crude literalism, as error typical of psychic preaching, the 'faith of fools'! For who are 'the dead'? The initiate knows that these are the psychics who have been deadened in this existence. What then concerns Paul in 1 Corinthians 15.12? He says that 'some' are saying there is 'no resurrection of the dead', that is, that the psychics cannot be raised from the deadness of this existence to spiritual life! For according to Valentinian exegesis the 'resurrection from the dead' is the 'recognition of the truth' spoken by those who have gnosis. (Pagels, 1975: 81)

In the light of the potential for multiple interpretations and teachings based upon Paul's use of language, even the words of Paul's letters could not in and of themselves be trusted to guide the belief and practice of the church. The letters of Paul and the words and deeds of Jesus were interpreted variously by many different groups. In this sense the early church agreed on the authoritative nature of Paul's letters. The practices of different churches, however, provided a basis upon which polemic could be built and different expressions of the faith could be distinguished from one another. The language of the traditions and teachings of the church were multivalent and difficult to control. As the writer of 1 Timothy notes repeatedly, words could be twisted toward one's own end. Indeed the letter writer's own practice of writing under Paul's name was a form of contorting the language and tradition of Paul toward his own theological and ecclesiological purposes. The language of the tradition could not be trusted to speak on its own, but the behaviour of people in the church could be described, managed and supervised. Christians could parrot a creed, but their public and private lives were much more revelatory of their true beliefs. Just how men, women, widows, slaves and children were behaving was a gauge of their appropriate indoctrination in the traditions of the faith. Gauging such behaviour was the work of the bishops and elders of the church, and it is to this task of oversight of behaviour which the letter writer calls the leadership of the church to greater vigilance.

The description of the church as the 'household of God . . . the pillar and bulwark of the truth', represents a remarkably dense and diverse combination of images. The concept of household evokes the writer's earlier delineation of the attributes of bishops and deacons in 1 Timothy 3.4–5 and 3.12. Here the authority in the male head of household's management of wife, children and slaves, parallels the description of the church as God's household. Such an overlapping of images serves to imbue the daily management of individual households in the community with divine authority. The hierarchy of authority from God to male head of household is seamless. This is particularly clear in the aside of the letter writer in describing the attributes of bishops in 1 Timothy 3.5, 'for if someone does not know how to manage his own household, how can he care for God's church?' (NRSV). The letter writer conflates the structure of the church with the structure of the patriarchal household. This exercise of power in 1 Timothy 3.15 is charged with divine presence and purpose. God is described as the paternal head of household to whom all leaders are subject and through whom all leaders receive their own authority as heads of their own private households. In his work on the social setting of the PE David C. Verner has noted this combination of social structure, ecclesial structure and theological meaning in the letters:

> The author of the Pastorals never addresses the subject of the household life of church members as a topic in its own right. Rather, whenever he introduces the topic of household life he does so in the course of discussing one aspect or another in the household of God. (Verner, 128)

The culmination of 1 Timothy 3.15 is a bold ecclesial proclamation. The household of God is the church of the living God, the pillar and bulwark of the truth. As in his other confessional and doxological formulae, the letter writer upholds a standard Jewish pietistic theological belief. God is living as opposed to a stone idol. Such a claim underscores the sovereignty of God. Given this confession, however, the description of the church (God's household) as a structure, pillar (*stulos*) and foundation (*edraioma*), is somewhat contradictory and jarring. How is it that a sovereign and living God (*theou zoontos*) requires such a fortified structure?

Throughout the witness of Christian Scripture there is an ongoing tension in reconciling the relationship of a sovereign and free God to a central institutionalized cult. In a classic text in Israel's scriptural tradition the writers and editors of Samuel-Kings struggled with this issue of divine freedom in the stories of David and Solomon's plans and constructions of the first temple in Jerusalem. 2 Samuel 7 takes up this issue in a prolonged dialogue between David and Nathan and the Lord.

> Now when the king was settled in his house, and the LORD had given him rest from all his enemies around him, the king said to the prophet Nathan, 'See now, I am living in a house of cedar, but the ark of God stays in a tent.'
>
> Nathan said to the king, 'Go, do all that you have in mind; for the LORD is with you.' But that same night the word of the LORD came to Nathan:
>
> Go and tell my servant David: Thus says the LORD: Are you the one to build me a house to live in? I have not lived in a house since the day I brought up the people of Israel from Egypt to this day, but I have been moving about in a tent and a tabernacle. Wherever I have moved about among all the people of Israel, did I ever speak a word with any of the tribal leaders of Israel, whom I commanded to shepherd my people Israel, saying, 'Why have you not built me a house of cedar?' Now therefore thus you shall say to my servant David: Thus says the LORD of hosts: I took you from the pasture, from following the sheep to be prince over my people Israel; and I have been with you wherever you went, and have cut off all your enemies from before you; and I will make for you a great name, like the name of the great ones of the earth. And I will appoint a place for my people Israel and will plant them, so that they may live in their own place, and be disturbed no more; and evildoers shall afflict them no more, as formerly, from the time that I appointed judges over my people Israel; and I will give you rest from all your enemies. Moreover the LORD declares to you that the LORD will make you a house. (2 Sam. 7.1-12, NRSV)

In the narrative of 2 Samuel there is a struggle between the idea of the sovereign freedom of God and the structured institution of religion through which the community worships and attains access to God. For the writer of 1 Timothy the tension of divine sovereignty and institutionalized religion is resolved on the side of institutional structure in response to the danger of 'other teachings' that misunderstand and misrepresent the truth. The apparent contradiction demonstrates the collision of the writer's theology and ecclesiology. God is sovereign. God is alive. The people of God, however, require guidance and structure. The structure hereby provides guidance for right behaviour and belief, much as church leaders provide such controls for the maintenance of their own homes (e.g. 1 Tim. 3.1-7, 3.8-13). In this sense the church under the letter writer's leadership has departed from the potential of socially egalitarian expressions found in the early pre-Pauline house church movement (e.g. Gal. 3.28), and has structured the church in such a way that it is socially defined by the structures of the Greco-Roman household. As such the letter writer has wed the patriarchal ideology of Greco-Roman culture and the Hellenistic milieu with the structure of the church. God is sovereign, and this sovereignty encompasses and blesses the power of the male head of household. The church is enfolded into this structure, and male privilege within both the church and the home is imbued with divine purpose and power.

1 Timothy 3.16b: A hymn about Christ and the church

After the bold declaration of the nature of the church in relationship to God, the letter writer concludes the unit in 1 Timothy 3.16b with another liturgical confessional formula:

> He was revealed in the flesh,
> Vindicated in spirit,
> Seen by angels,
> Proclaimed among Gentiles,
> Believed in throughout the world,
> Taken up in glory.
> (NRSV)

The confession is structured carefully so that each of the lines in the Greek text bears an aorist passive verb in relation to a dative object, in all but one case appearing with the preposition *en*. Each of the lines claims some portion of salvation history, though not necessarily in chronological order. The subject at the centre of all this activity is clearly Jesus Christ. This Christological focus is in keeping with the opening greeting of the letter from 'Paul' to 'Timothy'. In a sense the rhetorical effect of the passive verbs with dative objects places Jesus in the centre of both God's saving actions in him and the Gentiles and 'world's' belief in him. In other words, this aspect of the hymn makes plain the way in which Christ is the meeting point between God and God's people.

Some of the events ascribed to Jesus in the hymn seem to represent a canonical sampler of confessions about him. In particular the first and last lines: 'he was revealed in the flesh' (Jn. 1.14), and 'he was taken up in glory' (Lk. 9.51, Acts 1.2, 11) echo elements of Christophany that are not emphasized within the uncontested letters of Paul. Other elements of the hymn are less clear in terms of their traditional connections. There are difficult elements in the claims 'vindicated in spirit', and 'seen by angels' in the second and third lines of the hymn. To what aspect of Jesus' birth, ministry, passion, death, resurrection or ascension might these lines refer? The hymn may refer to the ascension to the right hand of God after his resurrection. Indeed, Paul seems to retain a liturgical remembrance of a similar presence of heavenly intermediaries at the ascension of Jesus in the hymn found in Philippians 2.5-11: 'Therefore God has highly exalted him and bestowed on him the name which is above every name, that at the name of Jesus every knee should bow *in heaven*, and on earth, and under the earth . . .' (Phil. 2.9-10). Angels in this sense would represent the image of the heavenly throne with angels in attendance. One way in which the verse may refer to the earthly ministry of Jesus could be in the presence of angels in the synoptic gospel traditions of the wilderness temptation (e.g. Mk 1.13, Mt. 4.11); or the presence of an angel at the tomb in Matthew's empty tomb tradition (Mt. 28.2). In either case the absence of any reference to the cross of Christ or his suffering in the hymn of 1 Timothy 3.16b represents a very different Christological emphasis than is found in the undisputed letters of Paul.

According to James D. G. Dunn the doxological confession is an early Christian hymn (Dunn, 808). Quinn and Wacker note the pre-Pauline Palestinian Jewish-Christian origin of the hymn regarding its parallels to apocalyptic visions of bodily transport from the earth to the heavens (e.g. Enoch, Elijah, Moses, Ezra, Baruch) and the use of these motifs by Luke in his summary of the passion/resurrection/ascension history of Jesus in the gospel: 'When the days of being taken up [*analepsis*] had drawn near' (Lk. 9.51) (Quinn and Wacker, 346). While such scholars are guided in their dating of the hymn by important criteria of historical method, the incorporation of the activity of the preaching of Jesus to the 'Gentiles' (*ethne*) and the coming of belief about him into the world (*kosmos*) seem to represent a later development within early Christian literature. This development incorporated the activities of the church into the telling of the story of salvation history. Indeed in terms of canonical Christian traditions such a claim about the church and its structural place in God's sovereign purposes of salvation alongside the life, death and resurrection of Jesus Christ resonates with Luke's construction of the Gospel of Jesus Christ and the Acts of the Apostles as a two-volume work. Both the hymn and Luke's two-volume work claim that the church's activities of proclaiming the gospel and promoting belief in the whole world are a part of the redeeming work of God in Jesus Christ. The hymn as it now stands in a letter purporting to represent the Pauline tradition seems also to resonate with Luke's presentation of Paul as the Apostle to the Gentiles (*ethne*). In this the PE writer and Luke seem to view the church's place in salvation history, and Paul's place in the history of the church, in similar ways.

The form critical assessment of 1 Timothy 3.16b as an early Christian hymn affords the opportunity to wonder how such a piece of liturgy would function and be experienced within worship in the first-century church. Quinn and Wacker offer a conjecture about the setting within which such a hymn, and its Pauline analogues (e.g. Gal. 1.24), would have been sung in early Christian worship. He notes that the PE writer used this hymn in the hope that his letter would be embraced as authoritative because it connected in his recipient(s)' experience with the presence and activity of the Spirit in worship.

> A hymnic composition such as the one in 1 Timothy 3.16b, as well as a doxology such as the one to which Paul refers in Galatians 1.24, must have been received as somehow authoritatively accredited or warranted, probably as inspired by the Spirit. Solemnly announced (sung) in public worship, the hymn had been in that setting recognized as coming from the Spirit. (Quinn and Wacker, 343)

In reading this portion of the letter it is not entirely clear how the writer intended to connect the hymn and the preceding instruction to church leaders. One similarity between the teaching and the confessional fragment is the tensions or opposites at work in both. Just as the church is described as a pillar and bulwark of a *living* God, contrasting freedom with structure, so too, as Bassler notes, the confession demonstrates paired opposites in alluding to God's work in Jesus Christ: Flesh/Spirit; Angels/Nations; World/Glory.

> The overall pattern is abbaab (a = earthly event; b = heavenly event). Moreover, each stanza has a recognizable theme: the first defines through the incarnation and the resurrection the two spheres in which the Christ-event occurred; the second documents the presentation of Christ and the message about Christ through the same heavenly and earthly realms; the third describes two parallel conclusions. (Bassler, 1996: 76)

Importantly, the letter writer refers to the nature of the religious confession as *musterion,* a mystery: 'the mystery of our faith is great',

(1 Tim. 3.16b, NRSV). This term often implies how the sovereign power of God presides over the death and resurrection, and the cross and glory of Christ. In Paul's classic meditation on this mystery in Philippians 2.5-11 the paradox of Christ's outpouring (*kenosis*) of his authority as one equal to God in order to suffer on the cross stands as a call for those in the church to model themselves on his humbling action. Individual members of the church are called to participate, through their behaviour toward one another, in the mystery of God's work in Jesus Christ. In 1 Timothy 3.15 on the other hand, the church is envisioned as a part of the mystery of the letter writer's religion. The activities of the church are described in the second and third pairs of the formula: *preached* among the nations, and *believed* in the world. These are attributes of God's work in Christ that are themselves a part of the mystery of God's saving purposes. Importantly, the emphasis of 1 Timothy, 2 Timothy and Titus has to do not with the evangelistic mission of the church ('preached among the nations'), but with the doctrine and traditions of the church ('believed in the world'). In this sense, the 'insider' instructions of the letter writer regarding right belief and practice in the church are envisioned as a part of the mystery of Christian religion and the saving purposes of God. The letter writer's focus, however, seems to have shifted from Paul's understanding of building the church among Jews and Gentiles, to guarding and maintaining the belief of the church in the world.

Protecting right belief in the world provides another potential function of the letter writer's use of the hymnic fragment in 1 Timothy 3.14-16. In this declaration of God's revelation in the flesh, among the nations and in the world, the letter writer affirms the revelation of God in human form, and thereby challenges elements of Gnostic belief that may be operative in the 'other' teachings he seeks to refute. Certainly the notions of spirit, angels and glory are judiciously balanced in the formula and the tension between flesh and spirit is held as a defining part of the 'mystery' of 'our religion'. In this sense, the hymn, while not original to the letter writer, provides him with a pedagogical tool for imparting the essential elements of the faith and a means of counterbalancing and challenging those 'other teachings' that would focus simply on elements of spirit, angels and glory.

1 Timothy 4.1-5: Polemic against opponents

The implicit teaching against Gnosticism found in the letter writer's quotation of the hymn in 1 Timothy 3.16 provides an excellent introduction for the writer's overt attack on those described in the upcoming verses in 1 Timothy 4.1–5. In the most general sense the letter writer attacks those who have an apparent ascetic practice of abstinence from marriage and who refrain from eating certain foods. More than any other place in the letter, the writer here provides specific content to his quarrel with the 'liars' that he elsewhere more generally defames. As such, this portion of the letter offers valuable material in the scholarly conjecture about the context of 1 Timothy and the letter writer's purposes in interpreting and representing the Pauline tradition in the ways he does.

The letter writer begins this unit with a remarkable phrase regarding the Spirit and an important evocation of the latter or 'future' times (*usterois kairois*). The notion that the 'Spirit expressly says' (*pneuma retos legei*) evokes a context of early Christian prophetic speech. According to David Aune in his work *Prophecy in Early Christianity and the Ancient Mediterranean World* Paul's letters contain elements of prophetic speech where he recalls oracles that he had either delivered or heard in the midst of his congregations. For example, in 1 Thessalonians 3.4 Paul writes: 'For when we were with you, we told you beforehand that we were to suffer affliction; just as it has come to pass and just as you know.' Here Paul and those with whom he ministered remember their prophecy of suffering, and recall that it has been fulfilled. In much the same way the PE writer remembers a prediction of conflict in the church that Paul or another person had issued and here attests to its fulfilment within the experience of the letter's recipients. The agent of this prophetic power is identified in 1 Timothy 4.1 as 'the Spirit'. Consequently the predictions bear the direct authority of God.

The declaration of the Spirit's prophecy in 1 Timothy 4.1 frames the future in an eschatological scenario - a scenario that differs from Paul's apocalyptic expressions of the uncontested letters. In 1 Thessalonians 4.13–18 and 1 Corinthians 15.12–57 Paul discusses the resurrection of the dead and the return of Christ. In both these texts the elements of Christ's descent from heaven, along with trumpet blast and the clouds, mark the cosmic event of Christ's return and the resurrection of the dead. In 1 Timothy 4.1 the 'future times' are marked not by cosmic transformation, but by ecclesial conflict: 'some will depart from the faith...' Where Paul marked the final days apocalyptically and Christologically, the PE writer understands the events of the end times more within the historical realm, and more in terms of the daily struggle for right belief and practice within the church.

Within the genre of pseudepigraphy the letter writer's casting of the activities of his opponents as happening in 'future times' at once evokes the distance of the recipients from the historical Paul, and yet uses the authority of Paul's wisdom and knowledge of the church to inform their own experience. Paul is cast as one who sees into the future with the help of prophetic oracle. He is a mystic, and a seer. He is one who by virtue of his revelation from God has special knowledge of and insight into the future. Imagine the comfort for the letter's recipients that Paul knew, even during his ministry, of the struggles they would one day face. Imagine their encouragement at the enclosed instruction that it was being providentially provided for their own particular crises and their own unique struggles. In all this the letter writer serves to encourage the recipients in their conflict with their opponents, and to promote the effectiveness of his own prescriptions and directives about how best to prevail within the conflict.

The practices of renouncing marriage and abstaining from foods could apply to a variety of early Jewish, early Christian and other Greco-Roman religious expressions. Many commentators see an early form of Gnosticism at work in these characterizations; however, we have no evidence of any early Jewish-Christian group which would have maintained these Gnostic practices along with an adherence to Jewish law and tradition. Some interpreters (e.g. von Campenhausen, 147–209) have postulated a late dating of the PE (second century CE), and posed that these practices and other elements mentioned in the letters (e.g. the '*antitheses*' in 1 Timothy 6.20) refer to Marcion's ascetic practices. In light of his doctrine of the evil God of creation and the alien God of redemption, Marcion refuted all aspects of earthly existence. In this he renounced marriage and the eating of certain foods (and the taking of wine in the Eucharist). In his late second-century CE treatise *Against Marcion* Tertullian enumerated the theological problems of such rejections and therein offers a glimpse into some of the practices of the Marcionites which seem to include a preference for fish over red meat, and a general drive to disparage the 'beggarly spirits' of the God of creation.

> You disparage the earth, although the elemental parent of your own flesh. As if it were your undoubted enemy, and yet you extract from it all its fatness for your food. The sea, too, you reprobate, but are continually using its produce, which you account the more sacred diet .... You hypocrite, however much of abstinence you use to show yourself a Marcionite, that is, a repudiator of your Maker (for if the world displeased you, such abstinence ought to have been affected by you as a martyrdom), you will have to associate yourself with the Creator's material production, into what element soever you shall be dissolved. How hard is this obstinacy of yours! You vilify the

things in which you both live and die. (Tertullian, *Against Marcion*, Book 1, chapter XIV, trans. Alexander Roberts, ed. *Ante-Nicean Fathers*)

In contrast to Marcion's signature division of the God of Jesus Christ from the God of creation the letter writer seems determined to affirm the Penteteuchal notion of God's sovereignty over the world and the goodness of creation (1 Tim. 4.3-4). Although it is not certain that the letter writer combats Marcionism in 1 Timothy, the contours of the practices he describes in 1 Timothy 4.3, and the emphasis on the integrity and goodness of God's creation, seem to represent some of Marcion's teachings and to rebuke his disdain for the created world.

In relation to other known early 'heresies' the letter writer's reference to his opponent's abstinence from marriage and certain foods is more problematic. Indeed far from ascetic practices, the activities of many Gnostic-like groups were close to libertine in character, although the description of their activities is often exaggerated in the writings of those who oppose them. Pagels cites that in the interpretation of Romans 14.2: 'Some believe in eating anything, while the weak eat only vegetables.'

> Valentinians did not refrain from eating meat sacrificed to idols. Carpocratians likewise understood themselves to be saved by faith, and considered all material things (food, sex, etc.) as indifferent, neither good nor evil in themselves. (Pagels, 1975: 45)

In a sense, this Carpocratian teaching resonates in part with the claims of the PE writer in 1 Timothy 4.4: 'For everything created by God is good and nothing is to be rejected provided it is received with thanksgiving, for it is sanctified by God's word and by prayer.' Given the tensions between what is known of Marcionism and various Gnosticisms, the precise identification of the 'other' teachings and practices named in 1 Timothy 4.3 with a specific early Gnostic or Gnostic-like heresy is so far impossible.

In his commentary on the PE Dibelius cites several texts in the PE corpus that focus on the beliefs and practices of those whom the letter seeks to oppose: (1 Tim. 4.1-10, 2 Tim. 3.1-9, Tit. 1.10-16, 1 Tim. 1.3-11, 6.3-5, 20f., 2 Tim. 2.14, 23, 3.13, 4.3, 4, Tit. 3.9-11). Taken as a whole, Dibelius notes that the texts paint a relatively consistent portrait of the writer's concerns: prohibition of marriage, abstinence from foods and spiritual enthusiasm. According to Dibelius, these practices indicate some form of Gnosticism; however, only the broadest portrait emerges from the writer's charges (Dibelius and Conzelmann, 66). In the light of these generalities Dibelius wonders if the letter writer is purposefully vague in his characterization of the 'false teachers' so that the letter could have a more general application and more lasting authority for his churches. In this assessment Dibelius notes that he is indebted to Walter Bauer's history of the development of the different beliefs and practices of the early church in *Orthodoxy and Heresy in Earliest Christianity*.

> The author [of the PE] attempts to characterize his opponents as broadly as possible, in order to create an apologetic *vademecum* for all sorts of Anti-Gnostic conflicts . . . . The forms which the polemic takes correspond to a concept of heresy just being developed. (Dibelius and Conzelmann, 66)

Dibelius's understanding of the vague nature of the characterization of the opponents in the PE sheds light on the current interpretation of 1 Timothy's preoccupation with generalizing and establishing the authority of Paul's letters for the church. The letter writer's appreciation of Paul's authority is clear. He writes within his name, and borrows from the conventions of the letter form to mimic his style of communication. The problem for the PE writer is the specific nature of Paul's writings and the extent to which they do not 'hold up' as broad doctrine to guide the developing churches in their various contexts in the late first and early second century. The solution to write in Paul's name and extend Paul's authority and applicability to his churches, therefore, required a more general approach. The broad description of Gnostic-like practices is yet one more contrivance that underscores the rhetorical purposes of the letter writer: to control the authority of Paul's letters and teachings in the promotion of his particular ecclesiastical structure and teachings.

It is not difficult to find in the extant writings of the Apostle Paul the seeds of the confusion about Christian marriage and dietary practice evident in this debate. With regard to marriage, in 1 Corinthians 7.8 Paul urges those who are not married already to remain single, as he is. Marriage is for those who cannot control their desire for sexual intercourse. In such instances, Paul allows, it is better to marry than to be 'hot to trot', (*purousthai*) and out of control. Paul demonstrates a code of conduct for the community that is flexible to different social situations, and yet is targeted to maintain a certain level of purity and sexual morality within his church. The same is true with dietary practice. In 1 Corinthians 8–10 Paul addresses the trouble in the community around the practice of consuming idol meat. Paul notes that the Corinthians may be free in the gospel to eat such meat, but that maintenance of the community as the body of Christ requires that some forgo their individual rights in order to uphold the well-being of the whole church. In Romans 14.6 Paul notes that it does not matter whether one eats or abstains from certain foods. Honouring the Lord, and giving thanks to God is what matters. In both marriage and dietary practice Paul's own teaching charts a course between the kinds of prescriptions made by the writer of 1 Timothy and the proscriptions of his opponents. Paul's teaching represents a different kind of instruction. Bound and determined to unite and build the church, Paul teaches an ethic of communal responsibility and sensitivity that enables those of differing practices (Jews and Gentiles) to practise the faith together. The writer of 1 Timothy and his opponents, however, preside over already constructed communities in which specific practices of the faith defined who was inside that community and who was outside. Maintenance of right practice, therefore, was tantamount to maintenance of the church. In this project, we can imagine how the writings of Paul, oriented as they were to ameliorating particular conflicts, would have been woefully inadequate to guide the church as a centralized institution. The letters were open to various reinterpretations and reappropriations. In this vacuum of certainty the PE writer appropriated Paul's name and style of communication and inserted his general instructions regarding right belief and practice for the leadership of his church.

1 Timothy 4.6-16: Instructions to Timothy

The letter writer returns to the direct second-person singular address in 1 Timothy 4.6-16. These verses open with a call to 'Timothy', or the leader of the church, to 'put these things before the brethren'. The referent of 'these things' is clearly the teachings found throughout the letter. The letter writer is drawing attention to the task of 'Timothy' to relay what has been written here to the church. To do so, the writer maintains, will be to be 'a good servant (*diakonos*) of Jesus Christ'.

The use of the term 'servant' or 'minister' (*diakonos*) for Timothy's work in relaying teaching to the church represents a fascinating development of the term in early Christian use. In 1 Timothy the term functions in a technical sense to denote an office, outlined somewhat in 1 Timothy 3.8-13. Deacons, like bishops, bear certain responsibilities in the church, and must adhere to a particular code of conduct within the community.

Earlier Christian use of *diakonia/diakoneo* connects the term to a more basic function denoting the table service of women and slaves within the household (e.g. Mk 1.31). The early church connected this practice, through various Jesus traditions of table service, to the more general practice of Christian ministry. The designation of Jesus in the gospel traditions (e.g. Mk 10.45) as one who came to serve rather than to be served drew upon this notion of table service (*diakonia*). In addition the development of the Lord's Supper tradition, and practice of the Eucharist, clearly played on this notion of waiting at tables and continuing with the ministry of Christ. In 1 Timothy 4.6 Timothy is cast in the role of such a servant with the phrase *diakonos Christou Iesou*, but the elements of his service are to place training and instruction, not food, before the community. The notion of his service (*diakonia*) has been rendered metaphorically from the literal carrying out of menial tasks of the household to the official leadership and proper adminis-tration of the church.

The content of the letter writer's instructions in 1 Timothy 4.6-10 are somewhat vague. Timothy is charged to instruct the members of the church to avoid myths and to train himself in 'godliness'. The term *eusebeia* is not common throughout the New Testament literature, but it appears many times in the PE, 2 Peter and early Christian texts such as *1 and 2 Clement*. It is an important term in Greek religious texts, and also is used by Hellenistic Jewish writers, such as Philo. Most generally the term means 'religion' or 'piety'. It is associated with religious practice as well as belief. In 1 Timothy 4.8 the letter writer contrasts 'godliness' with 'bodily training' (*somatike gumnasia pros oligon*). Dibelius has noted that this contrast may be intended to challenge certain Gnostic ascetical disciplines (Dibelius and Conzelmann, 68). Thus the contrast would cohere with the writer's earlier dismissal of those who forbid marriage and call for dietary restrictions in 1 Timothy 4.3. The letter writer admits that bodily training (*gumnasia*) can be of some value, but insists that godliness – in other words the letter writer's definition of the right practice and beliefs of the faith – is of value in every way. The letter writer may admire the discipline of his adversaries in their practice of religion, but he maintains that discipline is only of 'true value' if it is connected to the appropriate beliefs and practices of the 'true faith'.

The letter writer summarizes his instruction on training in godliness with a discussion of the goal of the faith. The use of the near demonstrative pronoun 'this' (*touto*) in 1 Timothy 4.10 most probably refers to the promise of the present life and the life to come which the writer has addressed in 1 Timothy 4.8. Toward this goal of eternal life adherents of the faith toil and strive (*kopiao* and *agonitsomai*). These Greek verbs denote work and are used elsewhere in the PE to refer to the contributions of the leadership of the church (1 Tim. 5.17, 2 Tim.

1.2, 2 Tim. 2.6, 1 Tim. 6.12). In their use the letter writer conveys not simply work, but struggle and difficult challenge. In a variant manuscript of 1 Timothy 4.10 these verbs are replaced with the even more pointed verb *oneiditso* which in the passive voice carries the sense of 'toward this goal we are reviled' or 'we are reproached'. In addition to difficult struggle this verb denotes external harassment and a climate of persecution. The difficulties of hard work, struggle and potentially even persecution according to the letter writer are the cost of setting one's hope 'on the living God, the savior of all people, especially of those who believe' (1 Tim. 4.10, NRSV).

This final division between all people (*panton anthropon*) and those who believe (*piston*) is important. In this division the letter writer reveals his understanding of the saving purposes of God in the world and the role of the faith and the church in that activity. As Paul understood God's saving purposes in Jesus Christ, all people, both Jews and Gentiles, were included. For Paul the challenge of this gospel, which he discusses at great length in Romans 9-11 was that Gentiles had been made heirs of Abraham, and included in the promises of God (e.g. Rom. 10.12-13). The notion of 'all people' for Paul, therefore, was a scandal of the Gospel and a hallmark of God's gracious and loving provision in Christ (Rom. 11.32, 36). However, for the PE writer the use of 'all people' is included as a Pauline element and the addition of 'especially of those who believe' qualifies the Pauline 'all' in a dramatically new way. In the letter writer's formulation, the church, the community of those who believe, is the place of primary and special salvation. In the letter writer's appropriation of Paul's voice, the church and the special function of 'those who believe' has been elevated into a new place within the understanding of God's work as saviour. Dibelius summarizes the transformation from Paul to the PE on this point well:

> The juxtaposition of 'all men' and 'those who believe' is indicative for the position of a later generation. For Paul all men are, theoretically, capable of becoming believers. The Pastorals are reconciled to the fact that the faithful represent only a portion of humanity. Thus the church is not just a preliminary form of the kingdom of God but already its substitute. (Dibelius and Conzelmann, 69)

The letter writer's address to 'Timothy' in 1 Timothy 4.6-16 offers an important glimpse into the pseudepigraphical construction of the recipient of the letter. Just as the letter writer evokes traditions about the Apostle Paul's biography and legend in order to authenticate his construction of 'Paul' as the writer of the letter, so too he connects with traditions regarding Timothy in order to establish the authenticity of its recipient. Timothy is that one who has been reared and trained by Paul on the words of faith. Just as he is called now to instruct, so too he has been instructed. Yet he is not Paul, he is (as Paul himself points out in Phil. 2.22) 'like a son to a father'. His commission to instruct and lead the community, therefore, requires some clarification. The letter writer poignantly lays bare the problem of the entire letter and larger corpus of the PE. While Paul struggled throughout his letters with the problem of instructing and holding authority with churches in his physical absence from them, the PE letter writer struggles with the problem of how to perpetuate Paul's authority in the wake of his death, and the competing claims to his legacy. The letter writer couches his teaching in the pseudepigraphical environment of Timothy's 'youth'. In addition he suggests that some may 'despise' (NRSV) or better 'look down on' (*kataphroneo*) him for that. In this depiction of Timothy the writer expresses the central problem of his church, namely, the problem of authority. In describing 'Timothy's' challenges the writer describes his own struggle to guide the interpretation of Paul's teaching, and thereby build the church on his interpretation of Paul's model.

The writer details the extent to which the example of his 'Timothy' (in speech, conduct, love, faith and purity, 1 Tim. 4.12) sets a tone for the piety and practice of the entire community. The emphasis of the unit, much in keeping with the entire letter, is 'good teaching'. Here again, words, and the power of words to falsely or truly communicate the faith, are at the centre of the letter writer's concern. In this sense, the practices of public reading of scripture, preaching and teaching to which the letter writer charges his recipients to give attention in 1 Timothy 4.13 are fraught with peril. It is for this challenge that Timothy has been 'nourished on the words of faith', and called to place the teachings of the letter writer before the community. 'Godless and silly myths' abound (1 Tim. 4.7), making the path of godliness and right instruction all the more narrow and difficult to follow.

In addition to correct speech, the letter writer is also aware of the parallel importance of correct behaviour. 'Timothy' is instructed to train in piety (1 Tim. 4.7). He is called to become for the believers a model in speech *and* conduct (1 Tim. 4.12). The goal of this practice is stated that all may *see* (*phanera*) the progress of behaviour in the developing strength of his hearers' faith. Finally, the letter writer promises that holding to such practice of piety and teaching not only provides a model for others in the church, but also provides the means for the letter readers' own instruction and ultimate salvation. The practice (literally 'by doing so') of holding to the writer's instructions, both with regard to right teaching and right behaviour, is held forth as the means of salvation for the recipient(s) of the letter and those whom he/they instruct.

Finally, the letter writer has constructed a notion of the church in which right teaching and right practice are more powerful than any single personality, or example of the faith. This is a shift away from Paul's fervent plea in the seven uncontested letters to imitate his example, even as he imitates Christ (e.g. 1 Cor. 4.16, 11.1). The shift is from the authority of an individual personality to an established set of teachings. The letter writer imagines that even the leader of the church ('Timothy') can overhear his own words, in repeating the teaching, and be instructed and thereby saved. In this construction the letter writer passes a proverbial baton from a notion of faith centred on the apostolic authority of 'Paul' the teacher/preacher, to a notion of faith centred on the content of the church's teachings and practices. Paradoxically the letter writer makes use of the apostolic authority of Paul in order to bring closure to the practice of establishing the church on apostolic authority alone. The teaching is established, it is now understood as a kind of catechism and the letter writer imagines the possibility that even those who are chosen to teach might have something to learn from the repetition and practices of this instruction.

In 1 Timothy (along with 2 Timothy and Titus) we can see the development of a canonically based faith. In moving from the authority of individual personality to that of established doctrine and practice the church is changing from Paul's conception of it as modelled on his personal example, a 'body' if you will, to something more akin to an established structure, a pillar and a bulwark. It is in this final sense that the writer of the PE and their placement within the Christian canon perform the somewhat ironic alchemy of transforming Paul's flesh, his personal example, into immutable teaching, the bulwark of truth (1 Timothy 3.15). Behind the polemic of the letter writer and his use of pseudepigraphy is a bold move to appropriate the authority of Paul and the traditions associated with him to construct the letter writer's vision of the church. Indeed, in terms of the ongoing historical reality of the church and its understanding of the tradition, the letter writer charted a course from which Christendom has not yet departed.

The letter writer introduces his closing of his direct address to Timothy (1 Tim. 4.13-16) with yet another nod to the physical absence of Paul from the church. In 1 Timothy 4.13 the phrase *eos erchomai* combines a temporal conjunction with the present indicative verb. In this construction the conjunction denotes a waiting period 'until I come'. In this way, the letter writer constructs a space where his instructions can stand in for Paul's presence. Now that Paul has died these instructions to Timothy no longer function as an 'until', but rather as a 'from now on'. To be the church that Paul founded, to be true to the purposes of Paul's vision for the church, the recipients of the letter are informed thereby that the following instructions are what Paul had wished for the church. They were issued to 'Timothy' to guide the church, and to keep the church strong in Paul's absence.

Following the letter writer's reference to Paul's absence in 1 Timothy 4.13a is a list of the church's practices of worship. These final verses of the unit (1 Tim. 4.13-16) form a trove of reference material for the worship life of the early church. The letter writer calls the recipients to attend to the 'public reading of scripture, to preaching and to teaching'. This list follows, as Quinn and Wacker have noted, the order of the first-century CE synagogue service.

> The synagogal *ordo servandus* certainly seems to lie behind the terminology and functions designated at this point in the PE, and the importance of the Scripture reading in that service can scarcely be overestimated, as the famous Orphel inscription of Theodotus says of the synagogue which he erected in Jerusalem .... The crisp, almost rubrical directives in 1 Timothy 4.13 remind one of the inscription on the floor of the Sardis synagogue where the reader was to take his stand: *heuron* (finding your place in the role); *klasas* (with your voice modulated); *anagnothi* (read out the Torah); *phylaxon* (keep the commandments you read). (Quinn and Wacker, 390-91)

The reference to reading (*anagnose*) which Quinn and Wacker translate as specifically referring to the public liturgical reading of scripture is used in a similar way by Paul in 2 Corinthians 3.14 to refer to the practice of reading and interpreting the Torah, Prophets and Writings which Paul designates as the 'old covenant' (*palaias diathekes*). Collins notes that the placement of this direction in relation to the references to preaching and teaching in 1 Timothy 4.13 indicates that teaching and preaching in the letter writer's understanding must be based upon the reading and interpretation of scripture (Collins 2002: 129). Collins's deduction serves to illumine and give content to the list of church practices. Preaching and teaching within the letter writer's church were based upon the interpretation of the tradition. This provides contemporary interpreters of the PE with an even deeper appreciation of the letter writer's concern to establish the soundness of this tradition and its authority and reliability in the preaching and teaching of the church.

In addition to the list of liturgical practices in 1 Timothy 4.13-16, the letter writer refers to the particular liturgical event of 'Timothy's ordination'. In that event, according to the letter writer, the council of elders laid hands upon the ordinands, thereby conferring the gift of prophetic utterance. The scene evoked in this remembrance is somewhat reminiscent of Luke's description of the laying on of hands on Stephen, Philip, Prochorus, Nicanor, Timon, Parmenas and Nicolaus for the purposes of table service (*diakonein*) in Acts 6.1-6. The difference between the events, however, is clear: in Acts 6 the laying on of hands is conferred upon those denoted as full of the Holy Spirit, and who will attend to table service so that the Twelve might continue to preach the word of God; in Timothy, the ordination is for those who will take over the preaching, and the liturgical event is understood to confer the gift of prophetic utterance. Between these two ceremonies, we may see a delineation of different offices within the letter writer's church. The leaders who received the letters of 1 and 2 Timothy and Titus would have been part of that group which had been called to the teaching and preaching (and now protecting) of the word of God.

1 Timothy 5.1-6.2b:
Instructions on Various Roles in the Church

Introduction

After concluding his direct address to Timothy in 1 Timothy 4.16 the letter writer presents a series of instructions regarding roles and offices in relationship to the church. These instructions take up the general treatment of people in relation to their age (1 Tim. 5.1-2); the definition and care of 'widows' within the community (1 Tim. 5.3-16); the compensation of elders (1 Tim. 5.17-20); and the relationship of slaves to their masters (1 Tim. 6.1-2).

Formally these instructions appear to be a set, but they vary tremendously in terms of detail and emphasis. In particular the instructions seem to have different constituencies in mind. Indeed, the list appears within the form of an epistle as instructions to Timothy; however, the instructions at one point seem to apply to all people as a kind of proverbial wisdom (1 Tim. 5.1-2), and at other points to extremely different classes of people (widows, elders and slaves). As such the unit may well contain portions of teachings that the letter writer is either representing wholesale or embellishing with his own touches. While the series of teachings may seem banal and devoid of theology, an in-between-the-lines reading of the instructions and their presentation by the letter writer affords an opportunity to hear the voices of varied classes within the letter writer's church. Moreover it allows us to see the ways in which the letter writer's construction of the ideal church has different social, political and economic consequences for different groups of people.

1 Timothy 5.1-2: General instructions regarding age

The image of the household comes into view once again in the teaching concerning the treatment of people according to their age within the community. Parallels to such teaching are commonplace in Greco-Roman literature and inscriptional evidence. This would be the comportment of any moral man, namely to treat elders with respect (men and women as father and mother), and to treat younger people with honour and dignity (as sisters and brothers). Hierocles in his moral philosophical work *On Duties* offers a similar list of expectations regarding the treatment of people according to their age:

> The person who loves his kindred must treat his parents and brothers
> well and, on the same analogy, also his older relatives of both sexes,
> such as grandfathers and grandmothers, and uncles and aunts, those
> of his own age, such as his cousins, and those younger than himself,
> such as his cousins' children. (Malherbe, 96)

It is because of such formulations of stock Hellenistic cultural wisdom
in 1 Timothy that Elisabeth Schüssler Fiorenza has characterized the
church of the PE as one that has been stratified by *age* as well as
gender lines. Such a structure, she argues, reflects the social relationships of the Greco-Roman patriarchal household (Schüssler Fiorenza,
1983: 288).

In 1 Timothy 5.1 the letter writer states 'Do not rebuke an older
man.' This teaching seems to indicate that the leadership of the church
must correct and instruct the congregation with sensitivity and care.
The term for rebuke (epiplesso) appears only here in the Greek New
Testament (save a few instances in Codex Bezae (D) when Jesus
'rebukes' the crowds). The term bears the notion of harsh or aggressive
striking out. That such a strong reaction toward errant elderly folks in
the church is possible speaks volumes regarding the work of 'guarding
the true faith'. Apparently those who err outside the church are not
accorded any such restraint. In fact, one might fairly characterize the
letter writer's rhetoric toward 'false teachers' and 'liars' throughout 1
Timothy as 'harsh rebuke'. Within the church, however, the rules of
the household apply, and each member is accorded honour and
respectful treatment according to their place within the 'family'.

The challenge the letter writer presents in 1 Timothy 5.1–2 is that of
teaching one's elders. Given the clear necessity of correct instruction
in the community, and the fact that bearers of that instruction (such as
Timothy) may not be senior members of the community, diplomatic
imparting of instruction is essential. The household is modelled on
what the letter writer understands as the sovereign wisdom of God,
and therefore each age and gender group are accorded their place of
honour. By engaging popular philosophical wisdom regarding familial
behaviour, the letter writer provides guidance through the quandary.

The list of constituencies in 1 Timothy 5.1–2 is balanced until we
reach the end. There, in addition to treating the younger women as
sisters, the letter writer adds the line, 'in all purity'. The term *agneia*
bears in its use a reference to sexual purity, or chastity. Such an
addition raises the spectre of an inherent masculine heterosexuality
within the letter writer's directions. The family model of age hierarchy
and honour provides for the repression of both rage ('do not rebuke')
and male heterosexual desire ('treat younger women like sisters, in all

chastity'). While such a provision may seem to protect young female members of the church from inappropriate sexual advances, it underscores the structural vulnerability of women within the patriarchal household. It also underscores the implicit violence that women endure as sexual objects and property within patriarchy. This inherent vulnerability to violence is well illustrated in the particular instruction regarding the classification and treatment of widows in the following section of the letter.

1 Timothy 5.3-16: Widows

In 1 Timothy 5.3-16 the letter writer addresses the situation of widows (*cheras*) in the church. The term *chera* quite literally signifies 'a woman without' or 'a bereft woman'. As such the term itself is attended entirely to the economic and social reality of women in the Hellenistic world. The term presumes that a woman who is alone is missing something. In order to be complete she is expected to be married, to have a husband.

The New Testament use of *chera* often bears witness to the social marginality of widows, their vulnerability to exploitation, and their neediness (e.g. Mk 12.40, 42, BAGD, 881). However, in relation to the discussion of widows in 1 Timothy, Paul in 1 Corinthians 7.8 and 7.39-40 provides a remarkably different treatment of the situation of 'women without':

> 1 Corinthians 7.8: To the unmarried and the widows I say that it is well for them to remain unmarried as I am (NRSV).

> 1 Corinthians 7.39-40: A wife is bound as long as her husband lives but if the husband dies she is free to marry anyone she wishes, only in the Lord. But in my judgment I think she is happier if she remains as she is. And I think that I too have the spirit of God (NRSV).

Paul offers the opportunity for women within the Corinthian church to live without a man and in devotion to God. Such a definition of widowhood radically challenged the cultural assumption that women required association with a man in order to have value or purpose within the world. No doubt the ongoing social challenge of Paul's teaching is one reason that the PE writer assumes Paul's name and mode of communication in order to control the responses the church made to these new social and vocational opportunities for women. In 1 Timothy 5.3-16 the letter writer carefully engineers a narrow definition of the station of widow within the church from all those who are generally without husbands, to those whom he designates as 'real widows' (*ontas cheras*). As such, while certain segments of early Christianity defined the term quite broadly (e.g. Ignatius), others, such as the PE writer, sought to control the designation and apply it only to the most destitute and bereft of women.

In recent decades there has been a flurry of New Testament scholarship regarding the location of widows within the early church. Bonnie Bowman Thurston (1989), Jouette Bassler (1984, 1996), and Stevan L. Davies (1980) have all mined the texts of early Christianity and the Hellenistic milieu in order to understand the impact of Paul's teaching in 1 Corinthians 7 on the social reality of the church. Indeed the apocryphal *Acts* contain many references to the social revolution wrought by the church's construction of a space and vocation for women to live without men. In the *Acts of Paul and Thecla*, Thecla's betrothed Thamyris asks two men in Iconium about Paul, who has attracted Thecla's attention.

> And Demas and Hermogenes said unto him: who this man is, we know not; but he defraudeth the young men of wives and the maidens of husbands, saying Ye have no resurrection otherwise, except ye continue chaste and defile not the flesh but keep it pure. (*The Acts of Paul and Thecla* 12, trans. M. R. James)

The social revolutionary aspects of Paul's teaching in 1 Corinthians 7 and the evidence of its effects within the writings of the apocryphal *Acts* are further magnified by the fact that within portions of the early church the term 'widow' was applied not merely to women whose husbands had died, but also to virgins (much like Thecla) who did not wish to marry. Ignatius of Antioch concludes his letter to the Smyrneans with an indication that virgins, and not merely women whose husbands had died, were identified as 'widows'.

> I salute the household of my brethren with their wives and children, and the virgins who are call widows. I bid farewell in the power of the Father. Philo who is with me saluteth you. (Ign. Smyrn. 13.1, trans. J. B. Lightfoot)

Paul's teaching that women could remain as they were (without men) was explored in a variety ways and places within the early church.

The socially revolutionary and broad definition of 'widow' within early Christianity provides an important background for understanding the PE writer's discussion of widows in 1 Timothy 5.3-16.

1 Timothy 5.3-16 suggests that the letter writer's church held a particular office for 'widows', complete with particular qualifications, responsibilities, vows and compensation. Therefore the writer takes great pains to delineate those who are mere 'widows' from those he

names as 'real widows' (*tas ontas cheras*). For the letter writer widows
are any women whose husbands may have died. 'Real' widows are
those women who are entirely bereft of family assistance, over sixty
years of age and who have been married only once (see the rules for
bishops and deacons in 1 Timothy 3.2, 12). The community, according
to the letter writer, has a particular system for 'enrolling' (*katalego*)
such 'real' widows, and this enrolment apparently must occur under
the overseer's permission. According to the letter writer, under these
guidelines, and these alone, 'real' widows are accorded 'honour'
(*tima*) or financial compensation (5.3).

1 Timothy 5.4 concerns the issue of the broader category of those
widows (*cheras*) whose husbands have died, but who have other
means to financial assistance through family (children and grandchildren). In this verse the letter writer discloses that in his community the
nuclear, biological family and ties of kinship supersede those of the
church. The writer declares that the children and grandchildren of
such women ought to 'learn their religious duty (*eusebein*) to their
own household first (*ton idion oikon*)' (NRSV). For the letter writer
the household of God is discrete from the familial household, and
financial resources are not held 'in common' as Luke ideally describes
the early church (Acts 2.44); rather resources reflect various levels of
wealth or class. What makes a widow 'real' is her lack of connection to
private households, to children or grandchildren to care for her. They
are those women who, being left all alone, set their hope on God
entirely (night and day), who offer prayer and supplication to God, and
who thereby demonstrate their worth for financial dependence on the
church (1 Timothy 5.5).

The characterization of a completely bereft widow, devoted in
prayer to God and service to the church, shows that the letter writer is
describing his version of ideal widows rather than 'real' widows. The
notion of making supplications and prayers night and day echoes the
letter writer's ideal descriptions of piety. Paul describes his own
prayerful devotion on behalf of his churches night and day (e.g. 1 Thes.
3.10). Also Luke portrays the widow Anna's pious presence at the
temple night and day in Luke 2.37 (Quinn and Wacker, 432). The letter
writer engages this ideal understanding of the widow to serve as a
construct to define more largely the patterns of authority within the
church. In 1 Timothy 5.6-16 it becomes clear that this ideal is not
constructed in a vacuum but in a context of great controversy about
the role and place of women within the church.

In 1 Timothy 5.6 the letter writer contrasts the ideal notion of
widow with a characterization of the anti-widow: she who seeks

pleasure (*he spatalosa*) and who, though living, has already died. The notion of self-indulgent luxury seems to suggest that the letter writer fears that certain women are exploiting their positions as widow and abusing the community's financial support. While the particular heat of the letter writer's rhetoric is bent toward these 'pleasure-seeking', spiritually 'dead' women, the responsibility for the overall situation seems to be laid at the feet of their families. In this sense, the letter writer seems to have two constituencies and agendas for these short verses. The first constituency is the widows: for them the writer seems to have an ideological agenda. This idealizes some women while making self-indulgent demons of others. The agenda seems clearly tailored to discredit certain women, to marginalize their position within the community and to establish a norm of widowhood that conforms to the writer's standards, in his words, 'so they may be above reproach' (NRSV). The second constituency seems to be the family members of widows. Here the agenda is financial. As the problematic widows are characterized as living in self-indulgent luxury, family members who do not provide for their own relatives deny their faith and are 'worse than unbelievers' (1 Timothy 5.8, NRSV).

In defining these two constituencies the letter writer seems less interested in correcting offences or challenging errant practices than he is in defining what is expected of widows and their families within the church. The characterizations of self-indulgent women and faithless family members pertain to people who would be understood to reside outside the letter writer's definition of the church. It is hardly likely that ones described as 'without faith' or 'already dead' would be within the reach of the letter writer's instructions. In other words, this rhetoric seems less concerned with bringing 'outsiders' into proper behaviour, and more concerned with controlling the behaviour of those who consider themselves to be 'inside' the church and who desire to adhere to its commanded behaviours and established social obligations. Once again, the letter writer's treatment of the subject matter reveals that the letter is intended for church leadership, for those who are inside the church and in step with its practices and beliefs.

The expectations of ideal widowhood expressed in 1 Timothy 5 are echoed in other early church literature. The second-century CE Asia Minor Bishop of Smyrna, Polycarp, writes:

> Our widows must be sober-minded as touching the faith of the Lord, making intercession without ceasing for all men, abstaining from all calumny, evil speaking, false witness, love of money, and every evil thing, knowing that they are God's altar, and that all sacrifices are

carefully inspected, and nothing escapeth Him either of their thoughts or intents or any of the secret things of the heart. (*Pol.* 4.3, trans. J. B. Lightfoot)

The rhetoric of Polycarp and the Pastoral Epistle writer reveals a supervisory posture of the church's leadership over women. As with the imbuing of the male head of a household with divine authority, the notion of supervising women's actions – even their most personal thoughts and emotions – serves to construct an environment in the church which privileges male social power. Women are not only the object of male authority and ownership, but also the object of the gaze of male authority. In no place, not even within the space of their own hearts, is it safe for women to resist patriarchal authority. Both the writer of 1 Timothy and Polycarp assume much the same kind of control of women's lives within the life of parts of the early church, and such control directly benefited the exercise of male ecclesial authority.

By narrowly defining the position of 'widow' in the community the letter writer seems to have something more than financial savings or appropriate piety in mind. Indeed, by limiting the office only to those who are destitute both socially and financially, the writer restricts the potential 'talent pool' for the position to a small number of qualified candidates. This constraining of eligibility is even further defined in 1 Timothy 5.9 where the letter writer demands that only widows be 'enrolled' who are sixty years of age or older, who have been the wife of one husband and, as he demands in 1 Timothy 5.10, who have birthed and raised children. While this last expectation seems somewhat capricious, particularly as having children in 1 Timothy 5.8 seems to disqualify widows in terms of financial dependence on the church, it does bear a connection to the letter writer's promise of salvation to women through childbirth in 1 Timothy 2.15. Only such women would be considered worthy of the position of 'widow'. By this criterion of eligibility, the vast majority of women in the ancient Hellenistic world would have been disqualified – if not by life circumstance, then at least by early mortality. The writer has accomplished a coup within his community by attempting to eliminate women with social power, physical health and financial means from eligibility for the office of widow in the church. In light of these considerations it seems fair to wonder if the letter writer's ideal ('real') widow is really a dead widow, or a nonexistent widow.

In addition to the primary criteria of financial and social destitution, 'real widows' must meet other qualifications. In 1 Timothy 5.10 these are listed in a string of coordinating conditional check marks: if she has done X or Y, then she qualifies. This list may well represent some of the activities carried out by widows in the early church; however, they are remarkable as a set of qualifications in that they show how such women would be thought of in the letter writer's community: 'she must be well attested for her good works, as one who has brought up children, shown hospitality, washed the saints' feet, helped the afflicted, and devoted herself to doing good in every way' (NRSV).

The list reveals, again, the letter writer's preoccupation with public opinion about the appearance of behaviour in the church. Rather than appearing as effective leaders, widows are to be appreciated and well thought of for their domestic and diaconal service. In many ways, the same demands made of women in general in 1 Timothy 2.10 are applied to widows here. The widow's office and duties are divested of their distinctive character in the letter writer's description of who should and should not be enrolled. The ideal widow in the letter writer's opinion is nothing more or less than his version of the ideal woman. In his construction of the church, women would hold little authority or place to challenge his position or that of other overseers.

As with the earlier contrasting of ideal widow and 'anti-widow' in 1 Timothy 5.3–8 the letter writer moves from his check list of qualifications to disparage younger widows and their activities. In 1 Timothy 5.11 the letter writer commands: 'Refuse to put younger widows on the list' (NRSV). His justification for this refusal is that these younger women tend to revoke their vow of commitment to Christ in this office by later wishing to marry. In this revocation, the letter writer claims, they incur condemnation. Whether the immediate source of this judgement is God or the bishop is not made clear.

Hidden within the command of 1 Timothy 5.9 and 5.11 is an important artefact of women's history in the early church. The letter writer uses the verb 'put on the list' (*katalego*) to refer to the way in which widows are defined and managed in the church. The activity of cataloguing or enrolling widows points to an official office of widows within the church. While much of the NT evidence refers to widows (often along with orphans) as objects of charity (e.g. Acts 6.1, James 1.27) there is evidence both within the NT and extra-canonical and patristic literature that indicates that widows also carried out considerable ministries within the church (Stählin, *TDNT*, 462–65). In Acts 9.39 Luke records the presence of widows at the death of the disciple Tabitha (herself likely a widow), and their duties of washing her body and mourning at her bedside. Lucian in his *Death of Perigrinus* relates that when Perigrinus was in prison a group of aged Christian widows and orphans would come at the break of day and wait outside the prison (Lucian, *Death of Perigrinus*, 12). These activities echo some of the qualifications for widows that the PE letter writer lists in 1 Timothy 5.10 (e.g. washed the feet of the saints, showed hospitality).

The language with which the letter writer describes the suspect 'younger widows' reveals his double-edged hatred for and fear of these women. Prior to detailing the horrible ways in which their activities are disruptive to the life of the community in 1 Timothy 5.13, the letter writer discloses in 1 Timothy 5.11 that in spite of the appearance of these women 'being without', they indeed possess a certain amount of dangerous power. Firstly, the letter writer commands 'keep away from younger widows' (*paraiteomai*). Curiously, many translations render this imperative in relation to the activity of cataloguing such young widows (e.g. RSV: 'But refuse to enroll younger widows' and NRSV: 'But refuse to put younger widows on the list'). The verb *paraiteomai*, however, appears elsewhere in the PE in 1 Timothy 4.7, 2 Timothy 2.23 and Titus 3.10 and is translated as 'keep away from', 'avoid' or even 'drive out' (see BAGD, 616). Importantly, two of these references (1 Tim. 4.7 and Tit. 3.10) issue the imperative in relation to shunning the teaching or influence of the letter writer's opponents. This verb, appearing only in the PE corpus in all the New Testament, is specifically reserved for the exclusion of only the most despised elements of the letter writer's critique. Consequently, 1 Timothy 5.11 is best understood as commanding the letter's readers not merely not to enrol young widows, but also to avoid them altogether, or even perhaps to drive them out from the church. Such a translation reveals just how dangerous the letter writer understands these 'younger widows' to be.

After issuing the command to 'avoid' or 'drive out' the younger widows in their midst, the letter writer offers his first characterization of their power. The letter writer's use of the verb *katastreniao* depicts young widows as filled with tremendous sexual power that bears destructive implications for the church. The verb *streniao* appears in Revelation 18.7 describing the vigorous sexuality of the great whore of Babylon who glorifying herself boasts 'A queen I sit, I am no widow' (RSV). But the letter writer also adds to the verb the prefix *kata* and thereby designates that the force of the young widow's sexual vigour goes *against* Christ (*katastreniasosin tou Christou*). This remarkably graphic characterization of the sexuality of young widows reveals the letter writer's fear of women's sexuality. On its own, without the control of father or husband, women's sexual power is, for the letter writer, a dangerous and destructive force. This power is clear in John of Patmos's characterization of the Whore of Babylon as one who continues her boast 'A queen I sit. I am no widow, mourning I will never see' (Rev. 18.7, RSV). Young widows of the church are perhaps most to be feared because in their vigour and potential sexual power they can stand outside the official control of the patriarchal household.

The letter writer continues to underscore his fear of the sexual agency of young widows in 1 Timothy 5.11 with the phrase 'they want to marry' (*gamein thelousin*). At first blush this phrase may seem to indicate that young widows wish to become a part of the partriarchal system, but the infinitive *gamein* appears in the active voice, perhaps denoting that these second marriages are far from traditional. Collins notes that in the Hellenistic literature men 'marry' (active voice), whereas women are those who 'are married' (passive voice) (Collins, 2002: 141). The active use of *gamein* in relation to women in 1 Timothy 5.11 and 5.14 may indicate that, along with their vigorous sexuality, young widows actively desire (*thelo*) marriage, and thereby thwart social convention and patriarchal authority by choosing their second mates.

After the letter writer characterizes the sexual and potentially transgressive social power of young widows in 1 Timothy 5.11 he continues to disparage their behaviour in a list of ills found in 1 Timothy 5.13. Contained in the rhetoric of this list is the letter writer's double-edged hate and fear of young widows. First, in 1 Timothy 5.13 he complains that young widows, ostensibly those who do not re-marry, 'learn to be idle' (*argai manthanousin*). The option that young widows could abstain from re-marriage is no doubt based upon Paul's teaching in 1 Corinthians 7.39-40: 'A wife is bound as long as her husband lives. But if the husband dies, she is free to marry anyone she wishes, only in the Lord' (NRSV). Ironically, the letter writer must use Paul's name and authority in order to combat a social reality that resulted from Paul's own teachings. Far from a life of agency ('she is free to marry whom she wishes', and 'she is blessed if she remains as she is') the PE writer seeks to nullify Paul's offer of social freedoms to women, conscripting them to the wishes of the patriarchal household. Women are to have no choice between marriage and singleness. They must marry and, contrary to Paul's teaching, the men they marry shall not be their choice (1 Timothy 5.11, 14).

In 1 Timothy 5.13 the verb *manthano* ('*they learn* to be idle') bears the sense of formal instruction (BAGD, 490), and thereby signifies that the young widows are being offered an alternative training to that which the letter writer would call 'godliness'. He suggests that they participate in an alternative system of belief and training that is outside of his church's control. Indeed, the widows' training endows them with 'laziness', which is a polemical term. An in-between-the-lines interpretation of the letter writer's use of 'lazy' shows that the young widows are not so much inactive as they do not serve his approved social structure and ecclesial purposes.

Examining the issues of power at work in the PE writer's use of 'laziness' (*argai*) seems particularly appropriate in the light of the verbs he uses to describe the young widows' behaviour. Far from being idle, the letter writer complains that the young widows 'go around from house to house' (*perierchoma*). Dibelius notes that such a description reveals the general work of widows within their office, namely the work of making pastoral house calls (Dibelius and Conzelmann, 75). As such, the young widows have the freedom to move from house to house within the legitimate ministry of widows. They possess the social power not to be bound to one household (that of their father, husband, next of kin), but to move freely between households in their ministry. The combination of this social power with their sexual vigour no doubt disturbed the letter writer and gave rise to his combined response of hatred and fear for the young widows.

Note especially 1 Timothy 5.13 which seems to bear the full weight of the letter writer's polemic against particular women within the Christian community, and to reveal most broadly what Luise Schottroff has identified as his misogynistic agenda (Schottroff, 69–78). In this agenda women are not merely to be managed for the benefit of the patriarchal system, but are hated as women when they resist this management. Similar to 1 Timothy 5.6 where the letter writer characterized the 'self-indulgent' widow, in 1 Timothy 5.13 he derides those who abuse the office of widow as those who go 'gadding about from house to house; and they are not merely idle, but also gossips and busybodies, saying what they should not say' (NRSV). Such descriptions bespeak a gratuitous distaste for the activities of women going about their business outside the strict confines of the patriarchal household. When women are 'out of place' male leaders may view them with tremendous disdain and derision. The letter writer reveals his desire to control the power of women within his community and to circumscribe their power to speak and thereby lead in the church. Within the letter writer's definition of their 'proper place' women are objectified as decorous, chaste, reproductive and silent (1 Timothy 2.8–15) and they are the objects of honour; however, once they step out of that well-defined place they become profligate, selfish, wasteful and chattering and are the objects of scorn. Either way women are objectified and their subjectivity is nullified. The dramatic difference in characterization between these different groups of women bespeaks the letter writer's view that women are women only when they occupy a very specific and prescribed place within the social world; otherwise they are monsters. As monsters they are to be hated, but also feared.

A contemporary parallel to the PE writer's rhetoric against 'young widows' can be found in the characterization of poor Black women in the US as 'Welfare Queens'. In the 1960s as President Johnson's 'Great society' programmes took hold and more impoverished people became eligible for federal assistance (primarily through Aid to Dependent Children), a rhetorical backlash developed in American culture that stereotyped welfare recipients as primarily unmarried Black women with too many children. In this verbal backlash Black women became objects of great disdain and fear. In her work *Black Feminist Thought* Patricia Hill Collins describes the nature of this war of words. She notes that Black women did not conform to White, male-dominated ideology. This dynamic echoes the PE writer's anxieties in his descriptions of widows. The intersecting issues of economic power and social freedom at play in both the contemporary and ancient situations are instructive about the war of words both in the ancient and the ongoing struggle for women's liberation.

> The image of the welfare mother provides ideological justifications for intersecting oppressions of race, gender, and class. African-Americans can be racially stereotyped as being lazy by blaming Black welfare mothers for failing to pass on the work ethic. Moreover, the welfare mother has no male authority figure to assist her. Typically portrayed as an unwed mother, she violates one cardinal tenet of White, male-dominated ideology: She is a woman alone. As a result her treatment reinforces the dominant gender ideology positing that a woman's true worth and financial security should occur through heterosexual marriage. (Collins 2000: 79)

Fanning the flames of the letter writer's disdain for the social power and mobility of widows in 1 Timothy 5.13 is a list of three verbs that describe their speech. Similar to the letter writer's description of the widows' laziness, idleness and 'gadding about', he labels their speech as 'gossip', 'meddling' and 'saying things they should not say'. While the first two terms seem to trivialize and gender the women's speech as frivolous, the third phrase discloses the transgressive power of their talk. According to the letter writer the young widows say what they should not, quite literally they 'speak things that should not be spoken'. They break the rules of the letter writer's church. They challenge his interpretation of the tradition, and his organization of the church.

In the Gnostic text the *Gospel of Mary*, the issue of the power of women's speech to transgress the established or 'orthodox' under-standing of the tradition is very much evident. In the ninth chapter of this fragmentary text Mary relates her vision from the Lord, complete with its Gnostic content, and Andrew responds: 'Say what you wish to say about what she says, I at least do not believe that the Savior said this. For certainly these teachings are of other ideas' (*The Nag Hammadi Library*). Mary's speech challenges Andrew's understand-ing of the Lord's teaching. It seems filled with 'other ideas'. Much like the PE writer, Andrew's concern is to preserve the tradition as he has received it. Moreover, the letter writer engages in disparaging women's speech, cartooning it, and he shows his disdain for the women. Furthermore in the third phrase, he shows his fear: far from idle talkers, the young widows threaten the very core of the letter writer's interpretation of the faith, and thereby threaten his careful construc-tion of the church.

Obviously, while characterized disparagingly as gossips and busy-bodies, the widows' speech is certainly significant and disruptive enough to the letter writer to merit his attention. In much the same way that the letter writer has earlier warned of the speech of errant teachers in the community, he here claims that these younger widows 'say what they should not'. Once again, the letter writer raises the issue of transgressive speech. He seems to equate the younger widows with the 'false teachers'. These widows are not merely silly gossips; their behaviour poses a threat to the letter writer's ideal construction of the church. Dennis MacDonald hypothesizes that these women are among the letter writer's opponents. The false teachers may have offered a vision of the church that allowed for and encouraged the leadership and teaching of women. In other words, the agency and authority of both the 'false teachers' and the 'young widows' seem to pose a threat to the letter writer's position and control of both the church and its beliefs. In this sense, the women of the 'younger widows' group present the potential scenario of a competing or alternate vision of the *ekklesia* as that envisioned and ordered by the letter writer. While his declarations may be seen as dismissive of women's place in the leadership of the community, his preoccupation with their activities and teaching may in fact reveal the remnant of a history of another, very different kind of church.

The letter writer offers his solution to the misbehaviour of younger widows in 1 Timothy 5.14-16: they are to marry, bear children, run their own households and thereby give 'the enemy' no opportunity to speak ill of the church. This series of infinitives (*gamein, teknogonein, oikodespotein*) provides the letter writer's desired control of women within his community. Note that the third infinitive (*oikodespotein*, manage their households, NRSV) ascribes power to these women within a carefully circumscribed space that is bereft of larger social power. Certainly as rulers of their households women of a certain economic class had power, but it was a power under the supervision of patriarchal control. Recall that earlier in the letter writer's delineation of the qualifications of the bishop (1 Tim. 3.4), he notes that bishops (who are men) ought to manage (*proistamenon*) their 'own households' (*ton idion oikon*) well. While women had some control over the affairs of their households, the ultimate authority of the home rests with the male head of household.

1 Timothy 5.15 also offers an ambiguous side reference to one of the letter writer's preoccupying concerns. The verb *ektrepo* indicates that 'some' have turned away from the church and have followed after 'Satan'. With this description the letter writer brings to mind his introduction of the letter (1 Tim. 1.6), namely that 'some' in the church have swerved from sincere belief, and have 'turned' (*ektrepo*) toward meaningless talk (*mataiologian*). In light of this connection, it may be presumed that the rogue widows of 1 Timothy 5.3-16 compose a portion of the letter writer's opponents. In any event, the characterization of their new allegiance with 'Satan' seems to denote the letter writer's sense that speech and conduct that do not conform to his specifications are utterly outside of the church and on the side of evil.

The final verse of the widow section has posed a challenge in the textual transmission of the letter and the history of its interpretation. The most authoritative manuscripts maintain that 'if any believing woman (*piste*) has widows (*echein cheras*), let her help them'. This notion, however, seems somewhat in tension with the earlier call for the support of widows and relatives by heads of households in 1 Timothy 5.8. Such heads of households would presumably be male. For that reason, apparently, some manuscripts replace *piste* (believing woman) with *pistos* (believing man), or (believing man or woman). The more difficult and well-attested reading of 'believing woman' seems to envision that within the community of the church there are women of financial resources who care for women who have been widowed, and who have been bereft of financial support. Quinn and Wacker suggest that such women may well have been widows themselves (Quinn and Wacker, 447).

The story of Tryphaena of Antioch in the *Acts of Paul and Thecla* is instructive about the role of wealthy women in the care of widows in the early church. After spurning the sexual aggression of Alexander on the streets of the city, Thecla is dragged before the governor of the city for a hearing. She is charged, but because a stay in jail might threaten her chastity she prevails upon the governor to give her alternative accommodation. The governor calls on Tryphaena, a wealthy widow within the community, to care for her. When Thecla's sentence of being thrown to the beasts is to be carried out Tryphaena and her company of other women escort the young Thecla to the circus. As Thecla endures her battle with the beasts, Tryphaena and the women cry out in a chorus about the injustice and evil of the event. Tryphaena's social power and status in the community actually play a role in preserving Thecla as Tryphaena, in her fervent fight for Thecla's safety, faints and the governor stops the circus.

> But Tryphaena fainted as she stood beside the arena, so that her attendants said, 'The queen Tryphaena is dead!' The governor observed this, and the whole city was alarmed. And Alexander, falling down at the governor's feet, said, 'Have mercy upon me and the city, and set free her who battles the beasts, lest the city also perish with her. For if Caesar hears these things he will probably destroy both us and the city because his relative Tryphaena has died at the circus gates.' (*Acts of Paul*, 8, trans. R. S. Kraemer)

As the narrative continues Thecla goes to Tryphaena's house and Tryphaena provides for her saying, 'everything I have is yours'. As Thecla stays eight days in the house of Tryphaena, preaching the word, she converts Tryphaena and the women servants of her household.

The legend of Thecla and Tryphaena bears witness to the kind of communities of women envisioned in the PE writer's instructions in 1 Timothy 5.16. As a virgin, unattached to a male head of household, Thecla would be called a 'widow' in certain parts of the church. The legend of Thecla and Tryphaena attests to the power of such communities of women to transgress social limits. These women tend to themselves; they do not require male supervision or guidance; they challenge the governance of male authority; and together they prevail against their unjust judgements. The legend offers an alternative vision to the social ideology of the PE writer. This is a vision of women with political and economic power networking with women of spiritual and religious power. Together they create an alternative community that is autonomous of male authority and resists male rule. The legend of Thecla and Tryphaena in Antioch seems to be the PE writer's worst nightmare.

In 1 Timothy 5.16 the PE writer seeks to designate women who are without men to a ghetto of widows. The letter writer calls for women of means to care for other women so that the church might not be burdened. As such the letter writer designates these women as outside the church's official concern. Ironically, it seems that such a community of financially interdependent women would undermine the letter writer's agenda to control such unattached women in their speech and activities. However, such a designation may be a part of his intention to relegate such groups as private, and to disenfranchise them from the church. Church resources would therefore be concentrated on the small number of women who would qualify as 'real widows' (*ontas cheras*) according to the strict standards of the letter writer.

1 Timothy 5.17-22: Elders

While the rhetoric of 1 Timothy 5.3-16 regarding widows can be seen as somewhat polemical, with a potential agenda of narrowly defining or altogether eliminating the office of 'widow' from the church, the rhetoric regarding the treatment of the position of 'elder' within the church takes on a measured and conciliatory tone. While presenting the process for redressing elders who persist in sin, throughout this section the letter writer assumes that the work of elders is valuable to the church and that the office requires judicious and impartial administration by 'Timothy' or the recipients of the letter. Therefore, even though the directions for widows, elders and slaves appear in this larger unit as a series, they reflect different agendas on the part of the letter writer. In this sub-unit regarding elders it is clear that we draw much closer to the letter writer's own constituency and circle of concern.

The most striking difference between the treatment of the widows and the elders in 1 Timothy 5.3-22 comes in the discussion with both groups regarding 'honour' or financial compensation (*tima*). In the section pertaining to widows the letter writer uses the verb *timao* in the imperative form (honour); however, in the section pertaining to elders (1 Tim. 5.17-22) the letter writer uses the noun form *time*, as he does in the section on slaves (1 Tim. 6.1-2). Some commentators explain that the letter writer sharply curtails the number of legitimate widow positions within the community on financial grounds. The call for families to fulfil their financial obligations to their dependent women is taken as an indication of a shortfall within the letter writer's understanding of the financial resources of the community (e.g. Collins, 2002: 143). Times were tight. Cuts had to be made.

This apology, however, soon runs into the contradictory evidence of 1 Timothy 5.17 where the letter writer exhorts that elders who 'rule well' be afforded 'double honour' (*diples times*), or extra financial compensation. One can hardly make a case that the finances of the community were stretched thin when such a merit raise is afforded to one group, while the rolls of the other office were being drastically cut. Clearly, an agenda other than economic scarcity is afoot for the letter writer.

It is just this kind of contradiction that thwarts the frequent claim that the PE represent the natural development of the church in a more 'common-sense' form than the church of Paul's seven uncontested letters. Such an assessment of the PE sees the curtailing of the office of widow as a 'necessary evil' when the church encountered the inevitable reality of the 'real world' in the face of the delay of the *parousia*. The problem with this interpretation is that it assumes that cuts in the church's leadership are free of ideological investment or political agenda. If we examine, however, the uneven treatment of compensation and concern for finances regarding the two groups of widows and elders, the allocation of money becomes a raw statement of the distribution of power within the church. That distribution, under the close direction of the letter writer, is made along age and gender lines.

In 1 Timothy 5.17b the letter writer discloses the various activities of elders. His encouragement about double honour is most especially (*malista*) for those who work in the word (preaching) and teaching. The office of elder seems to bespeak various activities that included, but were not limited to, proclamation (note the absence of any reference to the gospel as the content of the preaching) and teaching. The letter writer understands the work of preaching and teaching to be the most valuable according to the model of Paul, an apostle who both proclaimed and taught in the church. Note that the letter writer reflects the same hierarchy of duties in the church as reflected in Acts 6.1-6. Here the Twelve appoint seven (including Stephen) to serve tables (*diakonein*) (thus serving in order that they may care for the widows of the community), while the Twelve be allowed to continue to preach the word of God.

In addition to the importance of preaching and teaching in the traditions of the early church, these activities also connect with one of the letter writer's larger concerns. As noted earlier the letter writer is concerned to keep the religious language of the community pure, or without blemish. Toward this agenda the letter writer consolidates and seeks special compensation for those who preach and teach in the community. Preaching and teaching in this sense are not only elevated as activities of value in the community, but are also controlled by the authority that determines financial compensation and institutional privilege. Compensation for the work is to be centralized and systematized, thus controlling both who can speak with religious authority and what can be preached and taught. In this sense even the select few who are afforded 'double honour' are brought under the control and supervision of the ecclesiastical authorities.

The letter writer's exhortation to compensate elders is followed by a justification (*gar*) based upon what the writer identifies as scripture (*graphe*). The citations in 1 Timothy 5.18 combine traditions related to Israel's scripture (Deut. 25.4) and the sayings of Jesus (Mt. 10.10/Lk. 10. 7). The entire compilation, however, appears to be based on Paul's own references to these traditions in 1 Corinthians 9.9. Importantly, while the letter writer may be drawing on his knowledge of Paul's authoritative writings, his construal of the scripture references as justifying the compensation of elders entirely misses Paul's point that his voluntary service is an example for the Corinthian church. In this sense, the letter writer's engagement of the Pauline tradition seems less concerned with the personal example and authority of the apostle than it is with the written word in his letters (see Appendix 3). At the very least, the letter writer's categorization of Jesus tradition as 'scripture' alongside the Pentateuchal reference seems to be noteworthy. It signals the historical distance between the letter writer and Paul who indeed honoured 'sayings of the Lord', but referred to Israel's sacred writings only as 'scripture'. Indeed, the category of *graphe* in the context of 1 Timothy may well offer insight into the important role the Pastoral Epistles played in defining the nature of the early Christian canon. This role would be both to constrain Paul's seven authentic letters toward a particular understanding of the church, and to provide an example whereby the sacred traditions of Israel's Torah, Prophets and Writings are placed alongside the church's written codification of the teachings of Jesus.

After his promotion of the financial compensation of elders, the letter writer turns his attention to the judicial process for discerning wrongdoing on the part of elders and the means of taking disciplinary action against them. The system to which the writer refers is drawn from Deuteronomy 19.15: 'Only on the charge of two or three witnesses shall the charge be sustained.' This rule stands in Israel's legal code to protect one man from the possibility of malicious attack or personal vendetta. This concern seems ironic in the light of the writer's earlier caustic tone toward widows. While the letter writer personally attacks the character of certain widows as 'lazy', 'wanton' and destructive to the community, he requires adjudication of complaints against elders. Widows apparently are subject to ad hoc character assassination, while elders merit balance, objectivity and fairness. Once again, we can glimpse the social constituency of the letter writer when we read through the lines of his disparity in treating widows and elders.

In 1 Timothy 5.20 the letter writer announces the punishment for wrongdoing among elders. The letter writer announces the rule that elders who persist in sinning will endure a public rebuke (in the presence of all). The purpose of this rebuke is not for repentance on the part of the errant elder, but so that the rest (*hoi loipoi*) of the elders might be afraid. In other words, even in misconduct, the elders (as the bishops and deacons) have a public role to play. In their idealized conduct as leaders of the church and their households, they stand as a positive model for conduct and by their behaviour the esteem of the church is magnified. In their punishable conduct, they serve as targets of public rebuke, and their negative model instils fear (which presumably results in right behaviour) among the rest of the elders. In all ways the letter writer imagines that the public example of the church's leadership plays an important role in the church.

To close out the directions regarding elders the letter writer turns to second-person address to 'Timothy'. In 1 Timothy 5.21-22 the constructed recipient is charged with the impartial administration of these rules regarding officials, and is commanded to be careful in the work of ordaining such officials. Finally he is called not to participate in another person's sins, but to keep himself pure. While elders are subject to public scrutiny, the writer casts the recipient's supervision not only within the earthly realm, but by the heavens as well. As part of the letter writer's command, the recipient is reminded of the heavenly court of God, Christ Jesus and the elect angels watching his management of the church. While elders cannot hide from the supervision of the bishops, bishops and other leaders cannot hide from the supervision of the divine.

The imagery evoked in 1 Timothy 5.17-22 maintains a tension between an ideal vision of the church's leadership in which elders and bishops rule well, and the reality of the church in which charges are brought against church leaders, public rebukes are necessary to enforce an atmosphere of accountability and even 'Timothy' needs to be reminded to keep himself pure. This tension dramatizes the distance between the letter writer's ideal vision for the church and the realities of administration and leadership that challenge the fulfilment of that vision.

1 Timothy 5.23-25: Incidental advice and proverbial wisdom

In these two verses the letter writer's serial treatment regarding widows, elders and slaves in 1 Timothy 5.3-6.2 is interrupted with two different teachings. The first in 1 Timothy 5.23 is a prescription for stomach pain, and the second is some wisdom regarding the variable judgement and perception of sins and good works. Form critically the teachings are different. The stomach-pain prescription is in the second person, and appears to be a part of the ongoing ruse of a pseudepigraphical recipient. In this sense, it adds a note of authenticity to the letter format, encouraging 'Timothy' with regard to his frequent ailments. The wisdom about sin and good works is not included in this second-person direct address, and offers a generic teaching that couples an observation of the propensity of some sins and good works to be conspicuous and others that go unnoticed with an assurance that in fact all sins and good deeds will be accounted for. Indeed, both teachings are originally independent, and yet combined within the writer's address they make a humorous sense together that might not be apparent at first.

The call in 1 Timothy 5.23 no longer to drink (only) water (*hudropoteo*) but to take a little wine for stomach problems and other ailments seems to indicate a context in which the community practised abstinence from drinking anything but water. The letter writer critiques such ascetic practice elsewhere as a characteristic of those who had departed from the faith (1 Tim. 4.3). In the other direction, the letter writer includes in the list of qualifications for the bishop in 1 Timothy 3.3 that he not be a drunkard (*paroinos*). In this sense, the letter writer appears to be walking a middle line between ascetic abstinence that would to his mind deny the creative sovereignty of God, and the abuse of that created goodness.

The teaching on sins and good works or deeds in 1 Timothy 5.24-25 taps into the letter writer's ongoing concern with appearances and how things seem. The teaching stands in tension somewhat with the famous wisdom of Matthew 5.45 where Jesus teaches: God 'sends rain on the righteous and unrighteous' (NRSV). That wisdom upholds the notion that good things happen to both good and bad people. There is no accounting for it. It is a part of God's inscrutable and mysterious ways. In 1 Timothy 5.24-25 the teaching seems to hold some of this sentiment in its declaration that some who sin are not recognized as sinners and that some who do good works go unappreciated. This teaching, however, bears no sense of mystery in the doing of evil and bad. Ultimately, the teaching holds, both sins and good deeds will be brought to light. The tangible punishment or reward for doing evil or good is public recognition. The promise stands that bad and good deeds will be seen, perhaps not immediately, but ultimately. Behind this sentiment stands a social concern regarding adjudicating correct behaviour, but also a theological belief in God's ultimate purposes for good. While the workings of God's justice are not always apparent, the teaching holds that ultimately sins and good deeds will be exposed for what they are and for who perpetrated them. Socially this serves the letter writer's goal to maintain righteous religious practice, and theologically it conforms with his understanding of God's sovereign purposes for righteousness and justice. A strong doctrine of divine sovereignty, in this sense, serves the letter writer's agenda of socially constructing a community of righteous people. The message is clear, God is watching and accounting, and ultimately all people will be seen for their sins and good deeds.

The atmosphere of observation is once again evoked in these verses. Nothing is ultimately private. Nothing is ultimately secret. Nothing is ultimately beyond the realm of judgement or discernment. Such a claim both relieves and demands vigilance on the part of the letter's recipient. The relief is that his supervision is not ultimate. At the last, all will come to light. The demand of the claim is that even his deeds will also be subject to such accountability and public scrutiny. In the light of such hyper-vigilance a prescription for frequent stomach upset (and possibly ulcers) does seem appropriate!

The role of 'oversight' inherent within the episcopacy is behind the apparently disparate teachings of 1 Timothy 5.23 and 5.24–25. From stomach pain to the balance of good and evil, the writer supervises his congregation with complete authority. He knows all, and is in a position to adjudicate from the most trivial to the most ultimate concerns of his community. The writer's construction of a supervising authority in the voice of 'Paul' is ingenious in its completeness and effectiveness. 'Timothy' and all those who read this letter are under the gaze of this all-seeing and all-knowing pastor. While some may dismiss these verses as mere 'proverbial wisdom' the final verses of the larger unit in 6.1–2 underscore just how powerful, and potentially malevolent, such a gaze can be.

1 Timothy 6.1-2b: Slaves

This unit is the third set of instructions in 1 Timothy 5.1–6.2 that impart a command to 'honour' (*timao/time*): widows, elders and slaves. As has become clear, the financial benefit of the commands to 'honour' falls heavily upon the elders. In a sense, the bracketing of widows and slaves is a fitting enclosure for this social and financial privileging of elders in the church. Widows and slaves would represent two of the most economically vulnerable groups in the church. However, within the air of social freedom stimulated by Christian confessions like 'in Christ there is neither Jew nor Greek, there is neither slave nor free, there is neither male nor female' (Gal. 3.28), the groups would also represent areas of true social volatility. As seen through the examples of Paul's churches, Marcionite, Montanist and certain Gnostic churches, the early practice of Christian faith included a reassessment of social relationships. The place of women and slaves was being renegotiated in many communities. In Philemon, for example, Paul struggles with this new social vision in relation to the dominant society in his appeals on behalf of Onesimus. Elsewhere he commends women for service in the church (e.g. Phoebe as a deacon in Rom. 16.1). Such mobility among classes within the church no doubt created social problems and tensions. As representatives of groups most on the move within the church, women and slaves would have posed a particular problem for the letter writer. His construction of a church ruled by order and single-minded authority would require clear lines of social division and relationship. In a sense, the letter writer elevates the position and authority of elders through the social dislocation and submission of women and slaves. The rhetoric of 1 Timothy 5.3-6.2b is deeply scored with the tensions and strains of this social/economic construction of reality. Seen in this light, not one of the letter writer's prescriptions or proscriptions for behaviour in the church is benign or incidental. They are all a part of the larger construct through which certain members of the community are afforded social and economic agency, while others are called into the servitude of maintaining that construction of reality. Keeping this overarching agenda in mind, let us look carefully at 1 Timothy 6.1-2b.

1 Timothy 6.1-2b develops in two distinct phases. The first is a general injunction and the second lifts up a particular focus group within the church. In the first part of the teaching the letter writer's ongoing concern regarding the public perception of the church can be seen. In the second part of the teaching, the relationship of this concern to the enfranchising of his own social constituency can be seen. In sum, a good church is a quiet church, with leaders who are well-vested and well-served. Slaves, much like women, play an important, but completely subordinate role in this equation.

In 1 Timothy 6.1 the writer enjoins all who are slaves to regard their masters as worthy of all honour (*pases times*). This call seems to represent an echo of another pseudo-Pauline text from Ephesians 6.5, 'Slaves obey your earthly masters' (NRSV). In this citation the writer establishes his call for obedience on the basis of a theological model: obey your earthly masters, and your master in heaven will see your good service and return it in kind with blessings. Here Christian cosmology is brought into the service of maintaining the institution of human slavery within the church. However, in 1 Timothy 6.1–2b there is no such theological foundation. The writer simply states the bare structure of master's rule and slave's obedience, and claims its importance for maintaining the teaching of the church and its reputation. In this sense the letter writer seems to epitomize the 'Pauline' call for slaves' obedience without any urgency to apologize for the structure or to argue for its validity from within the Christian confession. Slavery is assumed, and its value for society – and for church – are assumed as well.

The term 'honour' (*times*) appears here for the third time in 1 Timothy 5.3–6.2b. Just as 'real' widows have been accorded honour and elders are to be afforded double honour (if they teach and preach well), slaves are called to honour their masters. In each case the term bears an economic element. In the case of slaves, however, the material benefit does not flow to them but from them. The call that slaves regard their masters as worthy of all honour (*pases times*) underscores that their entire purpose in life is the material comfort and service of their masters. They are to give themselves wholly to the service of their masters.

The second portion of the teaching in 1 Timothy 6.2 focuses this general call for slaves' obedience on its application in the life of the church. The letter writer demands that those slaves who have believing masters must not be disrespectful because their masters are brethren. This direction indicates that the renegotiation of social standing in the early church challenged the divisions between classes. One can imagine the practical dissonance of two people worshipping and confessing alongside one another as 'brothers in Christ', while they lived within a household as master and servant. In the face of this tension, the letter writer offers the rationale for even greater service by slaves of believing masters because those who benefit from their service are members of the same community, and therefore are 'beloved'. In other words, the letter writer takes what has been a scandal – the class divisions between master and slave in the church – and builds that reality into the justification for reinforcing that division all the more stringently. Where the early baptismal formula referenced in Galatians 3.28 and 1 Corinthians 12.13 envisions a unity within the church that eradicates ethnic, gender and class divisions, the PE writer calls slaves to manufacture a unity (through their greater service to believing masters) which buttresses class distinctions. In short, Paul's call for the church to be unified (a 'body') is evoked to construct a very different social system. For the PE writer unity becomes a tool not of social transformation, but of social coercion. Slaves in their happy, respectful, dutiful service to their masters are to be the glue that holds the church together.

As with the injunctions for women's silence and submission in 1 Timothy 2.8-15, 1 Timothy 6.1-2b has been lamented of late as leaving a terrible legacy of the church's role in perpetuating human bondage and degradation for 2000 years. The church has trafficked in the subjugation of persons in the pursuit of social and economic power, and has used the Bible and confessions as justification for such practices.

One powerful artefact of this legacy with regard to slavery can be seen in Cape Coast, Ghana on the western coast of Africa. There in the small fishing village of Elmina stands what the locals call a 'slave castle' constructed in the 1600s by the Portuguese. Throughout the period of colonization, this fortress was conquered and used first by the Dutch and then by the British. In the centre of the compound, which was constructed entirely of imported materials, stands a church. There the captains of the various colonizing powers worshipped surrounded by crowded, dark, putrid slave holds within which they bought and sold, brutalized, raped, starved and murdered men, women and children. Standing on the site smelling the centuries-old stench of the brutality committed there on humans one wonders how often 1 Timothy 6.1-2b and texts like it were evoked in those worship services to justify the Christian practice of slavery.

Given the horrors perpetuated by the church through texts like 1 Timothy 6.1-2b and in places like Elmina one might suggest that such texts and places be destroyed and divested of their status. Such an act, however, would miss the potential such texts and places have as unwitting witnesses both to the cost of the church's complicity with human slavery and the resistance of humans to such slavery. 1 Timothy 6.1-2b calls for slaves not to be disrespectful. Much as 1 Timothy 2.8-15 with regard to women's submission, these verses hold evidence that certain slaves were compelled by a different social reality in the church and were straining against the letter writer's prescribed reality. Much like the contentious women, they refused to respect the authority of a brutal and self-serving church leadership. Seen in this way, the text does not have to stand as a warrant for human slavery (as it has for so many years), but rather can offer a glimpse of the argument that was ongoing in the early church regarding how the Christian confession interacted with human social organization. In this argument the letter writer's voice (and his fervent concerns regarding other voices) rings tin-like against the hollow walls of his carefully constructed and idealized church. When the witness of such slaves is combined with the witness of the contentious women of 1 Timothy 2.8-15 one can hear over the letter writer's protestations a dissonant cry regarding the nature of the Christian faith and the character of the church. This is one way to hold such texts as sacred and yet resist their prescriptions and pretensions about God's intentions for human social relations within the life of the church. It is a way to participate in the argument that the church has been about since its inception, and a way to keep the argument going.

In addition to a witness of human struggle against oppression, 1 Timothy 6.1-2 also can function like evidence at the scene of a crime. It reveals the church's hubris, its false pride, and demands ongoing humility and moral vigilance from church leadership. Much as the church in the midst of the Elmina slave castle, this text reveals that the church has often served itself rather than the gospel and has committed hideous injustices and brutality under the banner of God's service. A text like 1 Timothy 6.1-2b stands as a sobering monument, much like the Elmina castle, evoking memories of the past crimes of the church and demanding reflection on where and how the church is complicit today in the suffering and exploitation of people.

1 Timothy 6.2c-21:
More Regarding the Opponents and Closing Thoughts

Introduction

The section of 1 Timothy 6.2c–21 engages the subject of defending the teaching of the letter writer 'Paul' from the teachings of others. Controversy regarding the teachings for widows, elders and slaves cannot, according to the letter writer, be tolerated. The letter writer then equates these teachings with 'the sound words of our Lord Jesus Christ'. Although the formulation is different, the reference to the words and teachings of Christ evokes Paul's practice in 1 Corinthians of asking whether he offers his teachings on the basis of the Lord's authority or his own authority (e.g. 1 Cor. 9.14 and 7.25). However, unlike Paul's uncontested writings, no particular tradition regarding Jesus' teaching from either his extant words or deeds can be found to agree with the letter writer's exhortations regarding widows, elders and slaves. Rather, it appears as though the letter writer has evoked the authority of Christ simply to bolster his teaching. He paints those who would disagree with him about the particulars of the church's social organization regarding women, elders and slaves as outside the Christian faith. Their teaching and practice is not in accord with the 'strong words of our Lord Jesus Christ'. Such a bald equation of the letter writer's agenda with that of Christ is startling, but through the adoption of pseudepigraphy the letter writer has already assumed the now elevated authority of the Apostle Paul. One must remember, the church was still very much 'under construction' at the time these letters were written. The letter writer's use of tradition is part of a larger argument about how to interpret Paul's teachings, and how to understand the structure of the church. This is not to apologize for his formulations, but to understand them within the contentious context in which they were written. Perhaps much to his chagrin, the fragility of the authority and structures he asserts as 'strong' is implicitly evident, as is the setting of controversy and dispute which occasions the writing of the PE. It is precisely because the words of Jesus Christ and Paul are fluid and open to interpretation that he must clarify and assert his understanding of the 'true' faith for his church.

1 Timothy 6.2-10c: Instructions regarding the opponents' teaching

The final clause of 1 Timothy 6.2 issues two second-person singular commands: 'teach and exhort these duties' (NRSV). Within the pseudepigraphical construction the addressee is clearly 'Timothy'. The imperatives recall the citation in 1 Timothy 4.11: 'These are the things you must command and teach' (NRSV). Form critically, the shift to second-person imperative may indicate that the letter writer has merely gathered the preceding instructions regarding widows, elders and slaves from various sources and here summarizes the collection with his own call to teach. From a rhetorical perspective the shift to second-person address enables the letter writer to underscore the importance of particular issues in the life of the church, and to evoke the direct authority of 'Paul'. In this case, the substantive use of the neuter plural demonstrative pronoun *tauta* meaning 'these things' has its antecedent in the issues regarding slaves, elders and widows enumerated in 1 Timothy 5.1-6.2b. The NRSV makes the connection between this demonstrative pronoun and the material regarding widows, elders and slaves in its clarification of 'these duties' for 'these things' (*tauta*). The letter writer wants to enforce the teachings he has just issued about various roles within the community, and how and to whom 'honour' (or pay) is accorded in them. It is these particulars about the social organization and financial management of the church that most concern the letter writer at this point. For the PE writer, in addition to correct belief and speech, the maintenance of these roles and practices is an important means of combating the opponents that he addresses throughout the letter.

The verbs 'teach and exhort' (*didaske kai parakalei*) are paired only here in the NT. Paul in his uncontested letters uses the verb 'exhort' often, but in the first-person plural or first-person singular. In other words it is Paul, either with his co-workers or alone, who exhorts his churches. In the case of 1 Timothy, the recipient(s) of the letter are called to do the exhorting. They are standing in for Paul. Just as the letter writer uses Paul's authority to 'teach and exhort', he passes on the expectation that his recipients will teach and exhort the church. The letter not only bears the teachings of the church, but also models the ways in which these teachings should be put forth in the community. It is an extension and projection of the letter writer's 'take' on Paul into the general leadership of the church.

In 1 Timothy 6.3-5 the letter writer takes up, once again, his characterization of those who oppose his presentation of the tradition.

Those who 'teach in other ways' and 'do not agree' with the letter writer are challenged as knowing nothing and being concerned with making controversy and causing trouble. This unit is a summary of the letter writer's most pervasive fears and desires as expressed throughout the entire PE corpus. In his characterization of those who would oppose him, the letter writer reveals much about himself, and his location in the ensuing war of words and battle for the Pauline legacy.

In 1 Timothy 6.3 the letter writer picks up on the exhortation to 'teach these things' from 6.2c and disparages those who would 'teach in other ways' (*heterodidaskalei*) or would not agree (*me proserchetai*) with the 'sound words of Jesus Christ' (*ugiainousin logis tois tou kuriou emon Iesou Christou*). In this brief clause the letter writer reveals the dynamic in which he understands himself to be engaged. There are things that must be taught (e.g. 1 Tim. 5.3–6.2b). And yet there are those who seek to teach 'other things'. This conflict between the letter writer's teachings with 'other teachings' echoes the reference to 'other teachings' in 1 Timothy 1.3. These uses of *heterodidaskeleo* represent the only uses of this verb in the NT. For the letter writer those who teach 'other things' pose the central problem. Teaching is his purpose, and he calls the recipient(s) of the letter to do the same (1 Tim. 6.2c), and yet his course of action is ripe for conflict and opposition.

The first appearance of the verb *heterodidaskeleo* in 1 Timothy 1.3 signals the reader of the letter that there is conflict within the church and differing interpretations of his teachings. By 1 Timothy 6.3, however, the content of the letter writer's teaching has been revealed. The letter writer, particularly in 1 Timothy 5.3–6.2b has promoted the teachings of the church as he understands them. The traditional understanding of these teachings is the promotion of 'good order' and 'right belief', but viewed from the perspective of social power, the teachings seem to promote the repression of certain groups (women and slaves) and the privilege of other groups (elders). Consequently, those who teach differently might be those who champion justice for women and slaves within the ministry of the church. If the letter writer's rhetoric dividing his teaching from 'other teaching' is read as a discourse of power, the social contours of the church's reality come into focus. This is not simply a matter of the 'right' and the 'wrong' confession of a creed. Indeed the church's understanding of its doctrines has always reflected political and social struggles. The power of 1 Timothy, 2 Timothy and Titus in their current canonical location is their natural and innocent appearance as 'Paul' (in the light of their pseudepigraphical construction). They claim 'Paul's' authority to assert the original and correct teaching of 'the church' and furthermore they define 'the church'.

When the letter writer's mask of innocence and claim to Paul's authority are unveiled the constructed nature of his war of words comes into focus. In 1 Timothy 6.3 the letter writer uses a term that he uses frequently in the PE corpus to establish the solid and undivided nature of the church and its tradition. The term 'strong' (*ugiainousa*) occurs often in the PE paired with either the terms 'teaching' (*didaskalia*), 'words' (*logos*) or 'faith' (*pistos*) (1 Tim. 1.10, 6.3, 2 Tim. 2.3, 4.3, Tit. 1.3, 1.9, 2.1, 2.2, 2.8). Elsewhere the term is used to refer to physical health and well-being (e.g. Lk. 5.31, 7.10, 15.27, 3 Jn. 1.2). Paul in the uncontested letters does not use the term in any way. In the larger Hellenistic literary milieu it is used primarily with reference to physical health. The PE writer's use of the term is quite distinctive and underlines his particular concerns and agenda. In a climate of bitter contention over the interpretation of Paul's teachings about the church the letter writer is dependent on words and their power. As 'Paul' the letter writer has special authority to assert just what are the 'words of Jesus Christ' and the 'teaching that accords with godliness'. As a leader of his church who struggles to establish his teaching over others, he hopes against hope that his words are indeed 'strong', 'vigorous' and 'effective'. His use of the term *ugiainousa*, therefore implies both his boldness to claim the words of the Pauline legacy and his insecurity that words may not be enough. In the face of his uncertainty the letter writer professes clarity and demands obedience. Far from a communication for a specific occasion, 1 Timothy assumes the purpose of a church manual of discipline, much like its near contemporary the *Didache*, or the *Apostolic Constitutions*. 1 Timothy masquerades as epistle, while it asserts its doctrine and vision of the church as the only, the one and the true.

Another hidden insecurity between the lines of the letter writer's claims about the 'strong words' of his teaching is the fear of contamination or disease. As *ugiainousa* generally denotes physical strength and vigour, its use with 'words of Jesus Christ' bears (bares) a wish for inviolability and the physical vigour of the letter writer's church. It is clear from his characterization of his opponents that the letter writer does not see diversity or debate as a means to strength. Instead he imagines the strength of the institution of the church to be in its unity and hierarchal order.

In addition to his implicit fear of contamination, the letter writer's assertion regarding the 'strong words of Jesus Christ' seems to betray another wish on his part. The phrase the 'words of Jesus Christ' is most probably a reference to the gospel tradition in general, rather than any specific text or sayings source. In her work *The Gnostic Gospels* Elaine Pagels has demonstrated that the diversity of the gospel tradition, much as she shows about the Pauline tradition, was a challenge to the establishing of orthodoxy.

> Before that time (in the first and second centuries CE), as Irenaeus and others attest, numerous gospels circulated among various Christian groups, ranging from those of the New Testament, Matthew, Mark, Luke, and John, to such writings as the *Gospel of Thomas*, the *Gospel of Philip*, and the *Gospel of Truth*, as well as many other secret teachings, myths, and poems attributed to Jesus and his disciples. Some of these, apparently, were discovered at Nag Hammadi; many others are lost to us. Those who identified themselves as Christians entertained many – and radically differing – religious beliefs and practices. And the communities scattered throughout the known world organized themselves in ways that differed widely from one another. (Pagels, 1979: xxiii)

In the light of this historical reality of the diversity of the 'words of Jesus Christ', the PE writer's appeal to their strength and unassailability reveals his deep wish for a uniform authority upon which the church can establish its teaching and exhortation. It is precisely to establish this authority that he brings his efforts to his innovative rendering of 'Paul's' voice in 1 Timothy, 2 Timothy and Titus. No doubt the process of canonization, in part, was an attempt to solve this 'dilemma'. Likewise in the interpretation of the canonical gospels, efforts like Tatian's *Diatesseron* (CE 170) sought to make 'one' that which was multiple and diverse. The PE writer was clearly not alone in his drive to manufacture a unified tradition in the reality of the early church's diversity of practice and belief.

In 1 Timothy 6.3-5 the letter writer employs stock Greco-Roman vices in a polemical fashion in order to characterize those who teach differently. According to Malherbe, lists of virtues and vices were a standard way to appeal to conventional wisdom within the culture, but various authors used them to reflect their particular views and concerns (Malherbe, 138). For his particular emphasis, the letter writer in 1 Timothy 6.3-5 highlights vices that connect with his prevailing concerns for 'right speech' and protecting the church from 'wrong speech' – for keeping the teaching pure. Importantly the letter writer's argument in 1 Timothy 6.3-5 is against those who teach differently. He is engaged in polemics with the leaders of 'other' ways of viewing the Pauline tradition and the church.

The letter writer charges in 1 Timothy 6.3-4 that a teacher who teaches things other than the letter writer's instruction is in disagreement, not only with the church's teaching, but also with Christ himself. The characterization of such a hypothetical teacher further illustrates the letter writer's ongoing preoccupation with speech. According to the writer such teachers crave controversy and are engaged in 'word battles' (*logomachias*). This compound term, appearing only here in the NT, graphically illustrates the heart of the issue for the letter writer. He is embroiled, along with these other teachers, in a struggle of interpretation about received tradition. Such a struggle of interpretation produces disagreement or disputes about what words mean and how they are to be applied to the life of the church in a new context. Disguised in Paul's own voice, the letter writer assumes a position of ultimate authority to interpret the words of the received tradition. From this vantage point he pronounces that the debate is closed. Here in this letter, in his words, lies the final, true interpretation. Such is a remarkably powerful cannon blast within the 'word battles' that surrounded the early church's interpretation of Paul!

From his position of authority the letter writer pronounces that those who engage in battles about words are subject to a massive list of ills: envy, dissension, slander, base suspicions, wrangling among people who are ill in mind and bereft of truth and, finally, imagining that piety is a means to financial gain. All but perhaps the last of these social ills represent some form of dissension or disobedience to established authority. Apparently, as 'Paul', the letter writer is above this fray; however, one might legitimately wonder if characterizing one's opponents as 'sick in the head' would not qualify as a form of 'slander'!

Notice that the problem for the letter writer is not so much the wrong words of errant teaching, but rather disputes about words. The very activity of dispute or disagreement produces disease within the church. This coheres with the letter writer's general sense that the church must be free from disputes. Women are to be submissive and silent (1 Tim. 2.11), children are to be well-behaved (1 Tim. 3.4), slaves are to be cheerful in their service (1 Tim. 6.1–2), and elders and deacons are to be above reproach (1 Tim. 3.2, 3.10). The letter writer's desire for civility does not represent peace, but a kind of social repression. His vision of the church is a tightly constructed ideal, with a rigidly established hierarchical authority that must be both above reproach and beyond challenge. Once again, the preoccupying concern driving this sense of vigilance against dissension is that the church's image, and therefore God's image, should not appear compromised in the broader public view.

The final wrongdoing in 1 Timothy 6.5 is peculiar to the list, and the subject of elaboration in 1 Timothy 6.7–10. Where the other problems relate to inappropriate speech within the community, the final ill relates to taking financial advantage from one's practice of piety (*eusebeian*). The vice of greed and dishonest gain were roundly disparaged in Greco-Roman moral exhortation. Malherbe cites Dio Chrysostom who quotes from Euripedes' *Phoenician Women* about greed being the most dangerous of vices. Following the citation of the poetry, Dio Chrysostom then offers his own summary of the vice. Importantly, he couples the vice of dissension with the vice of greed, much like the letter writer in 1 Timothy 6.6–10. But notice Dio Chrysostom counters greed by holding up equality. That is one social virtue, one Greco-Roman value, that the PE writer does not choose to emphasize.

> At greed, the worst of deities, my son,
> Why graspest thou? Do not; she is Queen of wrong.
> Houses many and happy cities enters she,
> Nor leaves till ruined her votaries.
> Thou art made for her – 'tis best to venerate
> Equality, which knitteth friends to friends,
> Cities to cities, allies to allies.
> Nature gave men the law of equal rights,
> And the less, ever marshaled against
> The greater, ushers in the dawn of hate.
>
> ... In this passage, then, enumerated all the consequences of greed: that it is of advantage neither to the individual nor to the state, but that on the contrary, it overthrows and destroys the prosperity of families and states as well; and, in the second place, that the law of men requires us to honour equality. (Dio Chrysostom, *Oration* 17.1–11, cited in Malherbe, 156–57)

While the previous problems in the list seem generic in nature, the letter writer's concern for greed most likely reflects a particular case or cases in his church. Just what that case may have been is impossible to discern. One might imagine that the writer is chiding those leaders from the church who have strayed from his teaching and practice of the faith, since the only teachers of the community who are in a position to make financial gain (*porismon*) are elders who are accorded 'honour' or payment (*tima*) for their service (1 Tim. 5.17). These being a relatively small group of men, the recipients of the letter may have known to whom the letter writer is referring. This final allegation regarding the disingenuous practice of piety for financial gain could in most contexts be considered slander against the moral character of a church leader. Once again, the letter writer is apparently above the fray of his own concern regarding contentious words and disagreement!

After the particular charge in 1 Timothy 6.5 that 'godliness' or the practice of piety is for some a means to financial gain, the letter writer focuses on the issue of money as a 'play on words' for 'gain' (*porismos*) in 1 Timothy 6.6. He states that piety holds great 'gain' or accumulation in contentment (*autarkeias*). Such a statement echoes Paul's own reflections about surviving scarcity of resources in Philippians 4.11: 'I have learned in whatever state I am in to be content [*autarkeias*].' Importantly, however, the letter writer is not extending this wisdom from his own personal experience, but rather as a general claim to which all should adhere. To this he adds some proverbial wisdom about wealth and its relation to life and death. He closes this section with general instruction regarding the relations of the desire and pursuit of wealth as a goal in life. Once again these general instructions may well connect with his specific complaints concerning his opponents or errant teachers in the church.

The proverbial wisdom of 1 Timothy 6.7 echoes claims made in *Sirach* 5.14 and Job 1.21. The tradition states the truism that humans are born without financial resources, and die without the ability to take accumulated wealth beyond death. As Dibelius has noted, this sentiment has parallels throughout Jewish and Greco-Roman literature as well as other literatures, for example Egyptian literature (Dibelius and Conzelmann, 85). As the letter writer applies this bit of wisdom to his context in 1 Timothy 6.8-10, he elaborates that the basic necessities of life, 'food and clothing', are sufficient for contentment. The traditions that reflect the ascetic practice of the Jesus movement agree with this view (e.g. Lk. 9.3). In addition the Cynic and Stoic popular philosophical notions of the simple, and therefore most virtuous life is echoed in the writer's sentiments about contentment and the simple life.

It is difficult fully to reconcile the tension between the material reality reflected in the writer's earlier calls for 'double pay' for elders, and for 'slaves to serve their believing masters well' with aphorisms that connect financial wealth with evil. To a certain extent, the writer seems untroubled by a class system in the church that would accord economic privileges to some, while demanding greater service and poverty of others. In addition, the writer is clear that it is not economic wealth itself that is the root of all evil, but rather the 'love of money' (*philarguria*). This same distinction is made clear by Polycarp in his letter to the Philippians 4.1 where he similarly declares the love of money to be the beginning (*arche*) of all danger. In this sense, the letter writer and other early Christian writers affirmed the stratified economic class distinctions of the larger Greco-Roman society, and called for maintaining the status quo within that established structure.

The letter writer's citation of the proverbial wisdom on wealth in 1 Timothy 6.10 may appear on first reading as a banal platitude. At the end of the verse, however, the writer refers again to those who have 'wandered away' from the faith and connects their errant ways with their passion for riches. In this connection the letter writer's class location and ideological agenda against his opponents are clear. Far from opposing wealth, the writer opposes 'class climbing'. He critiques the desire to have financial resources and social power one does not 'naturally' possess. Such striving produces social rifts within the community, and such rifts lead to challenges to the strict system of ecclesial authority that the letter writer seeks to establish. His appeal to wisdom and tradition (such as Paul's legacy) that portray this system as 'natural' and 'original' reveals the depth of his own passion to maintain his position of privilege and thwart the challenges of his opponents. Far from being a struggle merely about doctrine or practice, the letter writer's discussion of money clarifies the social and economic nature of the conflict in the church.

1 Timothy 6.11-16: More instructions to Timothy

Form critical commentators on this passage have noted that it intrudes upon the natural flow of material between 1 Timothy 6.10 and 6.17. The subject of wealth (*plousios*) and comportment with regard to wealth binds the verses. When 6.17 is read immediately after 6.10 the writer seems to be tackling the issue of those who would desire to be wealthy (v. 10), and then addressing the situation of those who already possess wealth (v. 17). The verses read as a progression of thought on the part of the letter writer.

It is difficult to determine why 1 Timothy 6.11-16 was inserted into these thoughts regarding wealth. As it stands the unit functions as an aside to the recipient which reminds him/them of the ever-present supervision of the letter writer and the expectations the church has of its leadership. The second-person singular address, 'but you, man of God' points a sharp finger through the general wisdom of the preceding verses. It is this kind of element in the letter which lends credence to its original setting being an 'in-house' ecclesial document not so much for general consumption, but rather for instruction of the leadership class of the church. While in form the unit may be an awkward intrusion, rhetorically it is a powerful reminder that the letter writer and his constituency oversee the behaviour of the letter's recipients. You, man of God, are being watched.

Many commentators note the potential baptismal and/or ordination liturgical setting of the tradition cited in 1 Timothy 6.11-16. The initial verses appear to be a charge to the baptized or ordained, while the final verses are doxological. The determination of the setting is founded primarily on the phrase in 1 Timothy 6.12 'when you made the good confession in the presence of many witnesses' (NRSV). Indeed the situation would hold for a service of baptism as well as ordination. In terms of the scholarly debate as to whether the tradition reflects baptism or ordination, one need only consult contemporary liturgies of these rites to see the overlap between the vows. As Bassler notes, however, the use of the phrase 'man of God' (*anthropos theou*) in 1 Timothy 6.11 narrows the application of the tradition to the leadership class of the church because it appears elsewhere in the PE (2 Tim. 3.16-17) in relationship to the teaching and preaching functions of church leadership (Bassler: 113). Also in the Hebrew prophetic tradition (e.g. Moses, Samuel, Elijah, Elisha and others) 'men of God' were those who bore responsibility for imparting divine revelation. Therefore, in the context of ordination, it is a characteristic of the priestly role, designating one as an intermediary between God and humans.

The limited context of ordination makes sense in light of the 'in-house' character of this ecclesial document. These are not merely generic expectations of every person of faith. The letter writer intends to evoke the recipient's sense of official duty and responsibility, and to remind him of the 'many witnesses' to his position, and the presence of those who oversee his conduct. In a sense this recollection of ordination serves to remind the recipients that they were called out by the leadership of the church, and that their current positions of leadership are accountable to that line of authority. The recipients of 1 Timothy no doubt thought of themselves, like 'Timothy', as faithful children of their spiritual fathers (1 Timothy 1.2). This reference to ordination is a way to recollect the importance of that relationship.

The call for Timothy to 'shun all this' in 1 Timothy 6.11 clearly refers to the prior list of social ills, including the striving for wealth, enumerated in the preceding verses. In contrast the letter writer calls for 'Timothy' to aim for righteousness, godliness (or piety), faithfulness, love, steadfastness and gentleness. The list, and its use in contrast to a list of vices, echoes Paul's enumeration of the works of the flesh and the fruits of the Spirit in Galatians 5.16-26. Rather than contentious and argumentative leaders, the letter writer envisions a church administrated by poised and pious men. This vision, however, is somewhat betrayed by the writer's charge in 1 Timothy 6.12: 'fight (*agnitsomai*) the good fight of the faith' (NRSV). The notion of an athletic contest or struggle is present, much as in Paul's use of the participle in 1 Corinthians 9.25. Here the work of church leadership is painted as contentious. Being faithful, righteous, loving, steadfast and gentle is a struggle. In the midst of church administration forces are at work that compete for the attention of church leaders. Against such forces, the letter writer calls the recipient(s) to 'fight'. In summary, the attributes of gentleness and love are called for in deference to higher authorities in the church; fighting and struggle are called for in relationship to those who adhere to other teachings and modes of administrating the church.

The sacred and salvation historical dimensions of the 'good fight of faith' are laid out in the next portion of the section. In 1 Timothy 6.12–13 the letter writer parallels the struggle church leaders have in maintaining their confession (and thereby the promise of eternal life) to the tradition of Jesus' passion, in particular his trial before Pontius Pilate (Mk 15.1–5 and parallels). In general the PE do not bear a hint of Rome's persecution against the church. The reference to Jesus' trial before Pilate in 1 Timothy 6.13 recalls Jesus' own teaching of his disciples that they will endure trials before kings and governors due to their confession of him (Mk 13.13). This track of imitated persecution and endurance emboldens those who hold to the confession of Jesus Christ. It holds their endurance with Christ's endurance, and it sanctifies their suffering with Christ's suffering. In the context of the letter writer's struggles, however, maintenance of the good confession has become an intramural affair. Rather than steadfastness in the face of Roman persecution, the letter writer evokes the good fight of faith as a struggle for internal church order and doctrinal purity.

In 1 Timothy 6.14–15 the letter writer shifts the salvation-historical scheme from the pole of remembering Jesus' passion toward the eschatological pole which anticipates Christ's second coming. In this expectation the letter's recipient is charged to keep the commandment unstained and free from reproach until the appearing of our Lord Jesus Christ. Again, the letter writer's prevailing concern is for 'right speech'. Placing his audience in the midst of salvation-history, they are portrayed awaiting the return of Christ. In this place their work is not envisioned as evangelism, preaching and teaching. Rather it is keeping the commandment 'pure' and 'above reproach'. In other words, the church's leadership is called not so much to mission as it is to institutional maintenance and doctrinal protection. It is the preservation of the church's words, its teachings and its practices, to which the church's leaders are called.

The letter writer concludes this salvation-historical rehearsal with a return to the theological and cosmological. The doxology in 1 Timothy 6.15-16 meditates, as do similar forms in the letter (e.g. 1 Tim. 1.17), on the sovereignty of God. God is above all, immortal and invisible. The letter writer is citing traditional liturgical material that would be familiar to his recipients. This formulation, coupled by the letter writer with the previous Christological claims, has the effect of drawing the largest, most ultimate authority around his instructions to the letter's recipients. This work of guarding the confession is presided over by Christ, and resides within the eternal reign and supervision of God. With such rhetorical innovation the letter writer seeks to fortify the church as the pillar and bulwark of truth (1 Tim. 3.15).

1 Timothy 6.17-19: Instructions for the wealthy

This final piece of instruction seems out of place after the remarkable benediction in 1 Timothy 6.15-16. Indeed the charge to the rich better fits with the instructions regarding money in 6.6-10. The writer uses similar terms regarding riches (*plousios*) as well as a similar theological foundation regarding God's sovereign provision over all life. However, the direction in 1 Timothy 6.17 seems to point to another constituency in the community regarding financial resources. Just as 'Timothy' has been charged to instruct church members not to climb out of their 'natural' socio-economic condition in 1 Timothy 6.6-10, he is called to teach those who are already rich (*tois plousios en to nun aioni*) to cooperate and fulfil their responsibilities to the community. Once again, these instructions reveal a stratified class structure within the church that the letter writer is keen to maintain. Just as those who do not possess riches are called not to strive out of their condition previously, so here those who are 'rich now' are called to be 'rich' in good works and to be generous (*koinonikous*). From both directions, the poor and the rich, the writer expects a primary commitment to the maintenance of the church community and its order.

The theological justification behind the letter writer's teaching is once again the sovereign provision of God. God is the one who provides all riches for our enjoyment (6.17) and supervises a future in which the good deeds (*ergos kalos*) provide a good foundation (*themelion kalon*) for those who perform them (6.18). The notion of quid pro quo of God's provision for those who do good deeds has a basis within Jewish scriptural tradition (e.g. Ps. 62.11) as well as in popular Hellenistic philosophy. The whole created order, as the letter writer perceives it, is ruled by the goodness of God, and thereby calls for the goodness of the people of the church. Such benevolence clearly serves the station of those who are now financially wealthy, but it also requires their vigilant nurture and care. Contemporary proverbs of the wealthy classes such as 'To those whom much is given, much is expected in return' are brought to mind by this passage. It is both a mercenary concept, and a means of demanding moral behaviour from the rich. In the sentiment the rich are secure in a well-ordered present, a stable social existence, and are offered a promised future life which, the writer assures them, is the 'real life' (*ontos zoes*). This future life is not based upon uncertain riches, but rather upon the eternal provision of God to which all should aspire.

As has been stated previously, the financial background to and the various components of the letter writer's instructions reveal both a rigid class structure, and an intriguing number of constituencies. Each group is called in some way to subvert their own immediate interests for the overall good of the community. A review of the message of the letter writer to each of the different constituencies reveals his own position and biases. It reveals that the good to which each are called is far from a common good. To slaves the letter writer evokes the good of not defaming the teaching of the church and the benefit of their believing masters (1 Timothy 6.1-2). To those who might aspire to climb out of their class station, the letter writer holds out the hope of not falling prey to temptation, ruin and destruction (1 Timothy 6.9). To those who are rich now the letter writer promises in exchange for their self-control greater riches in the 'real life' to come.

The inequities in the distribution of these elusive benefits evokes the same disparity observed earlier in the 'double pay' demanded for elders who preach well, as opposed to the silence, submission and pay cuts demanded for women and widows. The letter writer represents an elite constituency, and the recipients of the letter may be understood to belong within this group as well, and likewise be committed to the maintenance of the social order that ensures their current privilege. Paradoxically, the letter writer may understand his primary mission to be the protection of the church's teaching, but the closing instructions to the rich frame this project in his commitment to his constituency's financial situation. Such a concern is a helpful reminder that the church's belief and practices are always politically and economically involved, and that even the seemingly purest of motivations are connected to the vagaries of everyday material existence and class struggle. Though the letter writer might well protest, his own rhetoric reveals that the church's authority can never be fully separated from the influence of economic and social power.

1 Timothy 6.20-21: Closing salutation to Timothy

The closing words of the letter are directly addressed to 'Timothy'. He is issued two commands. The first is to guard (*phulake*) that which has been entrusted to him, and the second is to avoid talk associated with teachings that are 'falsely called knowledge' (*pseudonomos gnosis*). The first command states the overall position of the letter with regard to the teachings of the church. As has been noted earlier, the letter is not so much concerned with proclamation or evangelism as with maintenance and control of the church's teachings. 'Timothy' is called to guard that which has been entrusted to him. As an officer within the church he has been given a charge. That charge is the protection of the church's teachings. As the letter writer envisions his situation, the church is besieged by bad teachings, and the posture to which it is called is defensive combat. The second command underscores the prevailing anxiety of the entire letter which is that by even associating with the wrong speech, the church will become tainted, and believers will be lost to errant teachers and their beliefs and practices. Language has immense power for the letter writer. Words can bend the mind, and church members can be twisted away from the church's control by those who profess differently. This is not a climate of public discourse in which the best ideas are borne out through debate and dialogue. Rather, it is a climate of tight control and supervision over each and every word that is spoken and heard within the life of the church.

These final commands underscore the argumentative context within which the letter writer is operating. Moreover, they make clear just how important words were in the formation of the early church. Stone and mortar were not the essential foundation for the church; rather it was words. In the case of the PE it was the determination of the correct interpretation of the written words of Paul. For many expressions of the faith held Paul's letters in whole or part as essential, but these different groups interpreted Paul's words in radically different ways. As has been noted throughout these comments, these differences in interpretation led to a wide variation in the social structure of the church as well as in differences in practices of faith and confession. The letter writer, therefore, insists on control over the church's language and lays bare his defensive posture in the face of competing interpretations. In a sense the project of the entire letter has been the delineation of which words are the 'correct words' to determine the shape and mission of the church.

The command to guard what has been entrusted to him in 1 Timothy 6.20 evokes the memory of 'Timothy's' ordination once again (see 1 Timothy 6.12). In that calling and confession 'Timothy' was conferred with a sacred trust. That which has been entrusted to him is the church's teaching and leadership. As a leader within the church he is charged to guard and protect the faith. In addition, as its recipient he is to guard that which has been entrusted to him in this letter. His position, however, is far from unique. For while the letter writer addresses 'Timothy' singularly in 6.20, the letter's closing benediction in 6.21 is in the second-person plural (*humon*). This slip from the pseudepigraphical construction of private correspondence is remedied in a few manuscripts to the second-person singular, but the majority reading is clearly plural. While the letter has feigned an intimate communication between 'Paul' and his 'co-worker' it is clearly intended to be overheard and to instruct a larger circle of leaders within the church.

The phrase 'godless chatter and contradictions' in 1 Timothy 6.20 has long served as a focal point in the interpretation of the letter. The term *antitheses* appears in the writings of Polycarp of Smyrna (Campenhausen, 181), and is also used in the writings of Irenaeus in his polemic against Marcion. Such correspondence in use of the term has led some scholars to wonder if Gnosticism and Marcionism are in view in the writer's defence of the 'true faith'. Dibelius doubts that Marcionism is evoked in the reference to *Antitheses*, the title of Marcion's most famous tract, but does claim that the reference to *gnosis* is technical in the verse, and designates a particular teaching that the writer is combating (92). Quinn and Wacker likewise have argued that the use of the definite article in conjunction with *antitheses* denotes that the letter writer is not directly referring to Marcion's work by the title *Antitheses* (Quinn and Wacker, 559). Nonetheless, as a collection, the PE bear other marks of the anti-Marcionite struggle (e.g. 2 Tim. 3.16, 'all scripture is inspired by God'). The letter writer's preoccupation with maintaining the purity of the teaching and the indisputability of the tradition reveals the struggle of the late first and early second century about the interpretation of Paul, and the battle for legitimacy within the religious and political context of the Mediterranean world under Roman rule. The letter writer's unbending rhetoric reveals the high stakes in this battle. Within this climate there was no room for religious tolerance or pluralism. While plurality of interpretation was clearly the reality, the letter writer demands that the doctrinal line be hard and fast between that which is of God and that which is 'godless'.

The final verse of the letter is terse with its closing salutation 'grace be with you [plural]'. While such a brief closing might be expected in a private correspondence, Paul's private letter to Philemon contains more ceremony in references to others who travel with him (Epaphrus, Mark, Aristarchus, Demas and Luke). Generally Paul will often append 'the Lord Jesus Christ' or other titular formalities to his sending of greetings of grace (*charis*) in his letters. Consequently the letter appears to be quite skeletal in its representation of Paul's rhetoric. Indeed such brevity may anticipate that the letter was not to stand on its own, but perhaps be preceded by Titus, and followed by 2 Timothy. At the very least, the lack of attention to such formalities seems to indicate once again the intramural and select audience of the letter. As an internal ecclesiastical document it was intended for the direction and reproof of the leadership of the letter writer's church. As such its authenticity and authority would have been assumed and the audience would not require an elaborate ruse of Paul's style in order to accept the enclosed instructions. No doubt the letter's audience had heard these instructions before, but the imprint of the Apostle Paul's name upon the writing would have served as a compelling affirmation of the authority of what they had already been taught.

As stated before, the letter's ending is not on its own satisfactory, and seems open-ended. When the letter is read together with Titus and 2 Timothy, however, its themes are reiterated and the whole collection stands as a fulfilling declaration of Paul's final teachings for the church. Drawing on his legend, the letter writer assumed the end of Paul's life as a poignant moment for closing instructions to his co-workers 'Timothy' and 'Titus'. The collection as a whole would no doubt have been received as a trove of discovered wisdom, and its complete compatibility with the needs of the church's leadership of the time would have been seen as nothing less than divinely providential.

Epilogue
The 'Last Word' on the War of Words

The temptation after reading and engaging the constructed voice of 'Paul' in 1 Timothy for this commentary is to say something summative. After examining in between the lines of the PE writer's rhetoric I feel as though I should either finish the job and 'kill' the voice of the letter writer for good or 'make nice' and say I didn't really mean it. To return to my introductory metaphor of the letter writer as my distant, creepy uncle, fantasies of either ending seem plausible in terms of my family history. To be honest, in that history I have erred on the side of 'make nice' rather than fratricide. It has been my strategy of securing another invitation to dinner and remaining within the family. In many ways the work of writing critical commentaries on canonical biblical books seems to require similar etiquette. In order to ensure one's place within the conventions of scholarly guilds and ecclesial discourse, a delicate balance of critical and apologetic engagement of the text must be struck.

As stated in the preface of this book, however, this commentary has attempted to put forth a reading of 1 Timothy rather than an exhaustive and comprehensive engagement of its 'meaning' as a text. In this sense, while neither approach of 'murder' nor 'make nice' to conclusion is appropriate for this reading of the letter, some closing words seem to be in order. At least I owe my readers an explanation of my behaviour at this table of interpretation!

Much of my effort in reading 1 Timothy has been toward the goal of 'denaturalizing' the letter writer's rhetoric. By virtue of its canonical location 1 Timothy has posed for most of Christian history as the voice of Paul and the teaching of the church. In a sense my effort has been to qualify those entities of 'Paul' and 'church' as constructions in general and to demonstrate how the writer of 1 Timothy participates in constructing them in particular ways. The project of denaturalizing the writer's rhetoric has been oriented toward hearing both the letter writer's voice as a distinctive voice (rather than a general ecclesial authority) and to allow the voices of those whom he seeks to silence and marginalize to be heard. This agenda has borne obvious political commitments to women's liberation and human freedom, but it has also been bent toward troubling assumptions about the make-up of 'the church' both historically and contemporarily. The goal of this troubling has not been simply to make trouble, but to make room by virtue of demonstrating the complex and heterogeneous nature of the church of the PE writer and by extension perhaps our churches today. There is more to these communities than meets the eye. Attending to and caring for this complexity (rather than simply seeking to silence it) is a way to lead the church. The PE writer and I obviously disagree about this approach to ecclesial leadership, and yet I hope to have demonstrated the ancient nature of this disagreement embedded within the very lines of his own text. In a sense this disagreement is as ancient as the church itself.

In addition to 'denaturalizing' the rhetoric of the PE writer, I have also attempted to show through this reading of 1 Timothy how alive the text has been within popular and ecclesial discourse. This project has been to demonstrate the legacy of 1 Timothy's interpretation (for good and for ill). Progressive expressions of the church tend to ignore the PE and conserving expressions tend to assert these texts as norms. Both approaches miss the opportunity to understand the texts contextually and thereby learn about what the church has yearned for and accomplished in history. Women, children, homosexuals, slaves all have borne a particular burden as a result of these missed opportunities. Ecclesial leaders have missed the opportunity to appreciate how the church's structures are negotiated in history and are not 'natural'. Such a view of the church may seem to 'relativize' its authority, but in my assessment it renders it more ethically account-able. The church we have, whether we base it on 1 Timothy or not, is the church we make. The history of the church, whether based on the interpretive legacy of 1 Timothy or not, is a history within which we participate and for which we are responsible.

Finally, this reading of 1 Timothy has sought to suggest that different constructions than those of the letter writer of church and human social reality are possible. As such this commentary on the text has been self-consciously heretical in that it has been proposed as 'another way' (heresy). The war that the writer of 1 Timothy wages on the words and characters of his opponents is a struggle bent upon the assertion of a unitary construction of the church's authority as 'true' in opposition to the 'other ways' that are 'false'. Such rhetoric is very much a part of the church's history and contemporary reality; however it is not the only way to be the church. As this reading of 1 Timothy has attempted to unmask the letter writer's promotion of an oppositional view of the ecclesial life ('us' against 'them'), it has also promoted a means of ecclesial discourse that may be contentious but not necessarily oppositional. It has sought to imagine a reading of 1 Timothy that opens up the heterodox reality of the church's make-up and structures of power without resolving that complexity into declarations of what is 'true' and 'false'. While such a project results in less assurance of being on the 'right side' of a particular battle, it does provide at least the solace that we may continue to argue around the table in good, if not also strange, company.

Appendix 1
A Syllabus for a Course entitled: 'Following Paul: Authority, Church and Mission in the Canonical and Non-Canonical Interpreters of Paul'

Fall 2002
Eden Theological Seminary
Deborah Krause

Description

This course takes up the complex historical, ecclesial and canonical problems around the pseudepigraphical and legendary traditions that draw upon the authority of the Apostle Paul. The texts of Ephesians, Colossians, 1 and 2 Timothy and Titus, as well as the narrative of Acts, and various extra-canonical texts will be interpreted to discern how early churches interpreted Paul's letters in various ways as they struggled to define the role of the church in the world. In this vein the pseudepigraphical and legendary traditions provide a basis for exploring contemporary struggles within the church regarding scriptural authority, ecclesiology and mission.

Goals and objectives

The goals of this course are to gain an appreciation for the diversity of interpretations that arose out of following Paul, and to employ this diversity as a means for reflecting on the nature and mission of the church both historically and contemporarily. The following objectives relate to meeting these goals:

1. To articulate a claim about Paul's most central teachings regarding the church and its mission, and to discern how that claim both resonates and competes with other claims.
2. To read and interpret the various pseudepigraphical and legendary interpretations of Paul and to understand them within their historical contexts.
3. To engage contemporary debates over the nature of the church and its mission in the world, and to discern how these debates take up the interpretation of Paul.
4. To gain an appreciation of the complexity of authority, tradition

and canon in defining the mission and life of the church, and to develop skills in navigating this complexity toward the articulation of the church's mission and the living out of this mission in ministry. In this final sense the course seeks to develop for each student a sense of apologetics in discussing the church and its mission.

Assignments

1. Write a 3-5 page paper on your assessment of Paul's most important claims about the church and its mission. Select a variety of texts from Paul's letter's that back up your claims. Outline some criteria or method for selecting (and neglecting) the texts you have in order to make a coherent ecclesiology/ missiology out of Paul. We will share and discuss these papers in class. Please bring a copy for each participant in the seminar. **(Due 30 September)*****

2. Maintenance of a Following Paul journal in which you engage assigned questions about the primary texts, and you reflect upon secondary resources. **(Due 9 December)*****

3. An in-class presentation on a particular issue or theme in the interpretation of Paul in both an ancient and contemporary context. On the day of the presentation the student(s) will provide leadership for the seminar discussion of the primary and secondary texts from the assigned ancient context. **(Date TBA)*****

4. A 15-page research and exegetical paper in which the student describes both an ancient community and a contemporary community's attempt to 'follow Paul' on a particular theme or issue and thereby to define and live out the mission of the church in the world. It is hoped that while this paper is focused on a particular issue, theme or doctrine within the church, it will serve as a basis for the student to begin to articulate her/his own ecclesiology and missiology as he/she is engaged in the interpretation of Paul. **(Due 16 December)*****

*****   **It is expected that all written and presented work will abide by the guidelines of the Academic Honor Code found in the Policy Manual.**

Schedule

9 September: Introduction – The Quandary of Following Paul

16 September: Paul
Read: 1 Thessalonians, Galatians and Romans

> **Elizabeth Castelli, *Imitating Paul: A Discourse of Power* (Louisville: W/JKP, 1991), pp. 21-33

> Calvin J. Roetzel, *The Letters of Paul: Conversations in Context* (Louisville: W/JKP, 1998), pp. 6-78; 119-32 (use the outlines in pp. 79-118 as an overview for your reading of the letters). You may also find it helpful to review your notes from the course in New Testament introduction that you took, or other pertinent readings from that course or a seminar on Paul (if you have taken one). The point of this secondary reading is to enhance your reading of Paul's letters.

Journal questions
Where in these letters does Paul speak of himself, and in what ways does he describe himself? What are some of the conflicts and issues that seem to be at stake in Paul's ministry? How does this begin to help you see his sense of ministry and the church's mission? Focus on a specific text and discuss Paul's vision of the church and its mission.

23 September: Paul
Read: 1 and 2 Corinthians, Philippians, Philemon

> **Helmut Koester, 'Γνῶμαι Διάφοραι: The Origin and Nature of Diversification in the History of Early Christianity', in *Harvard Theological Review* 58 (1965), pp. 279-318

Journal questions
This is a challenging article with some technical language in it. Hang in there and look for the major thesis and the way in which it engages with the interpretation of Paul. What is Koester's basic point about early Christianity? Cite and describe several texts where you see Paul's letters showing evidence of the kinds of diversity that Koester describes. How does this view of early Christianity conform or conflict with your understanding of the early church?

30 September: Class Roundtable on Paul's Ecclesiology and Missiology (your 3-5 page paper on Paul is due at the beginning of class. Please bring a copy for each participant in the seminar)

7 October: The Historical-Cultural-Social Setting of Late First and Second-Century Christianity – The Problem and Necessity of Following Paul
Read:

> Roetzel *The Letters of Paul*, pp. 133-60
>
> **Raymond Brown, 'The Sub-Apostolic Era in the New Testament', in *The Churches the Apostles Left Behind* (New York: Paulist Press, 1984), pp. 13-30
>
> Elisabeth Schüssler Fiorenza, *In Memory of Her: A Feminist-Theological Reconstruction of Christian Origins* (New York: Crossroad, 1983), pp. 251-84
>
> **Martin Rist, 'Pseudepigraphy and the Early Christians', in David E. Aune (ed), *Studies in New Testament and Early Christian Literature*, (Leiden: Brill, 1972) pp. 75-91

Journal questions
How does Brown characterize the 'sub-apostolic era' of the NT? What points of contact and tension do you see with Koester's outline of early Christian diversification? How might you describe Brown's notion of the church and its 'development' in contrast to Koester's? How does Fiorenza's piece on the church after Paul inform your understanding of the 'development' of early Christianity?

14 October: Paul according to Luke
Read: The Acts of the Apostles, particularly chapters 9-28

> Your NT Introduction about Luke-Acts (e.g. Perrin and Duling, pp. 366-403)

Journal questions
Who is Paul to Luke?
   What tensions do you see between Luke's presentation and Paul's own descriptions of himself and his mission within Paul's own writings? Focus on one particular text in which you can detect Luke 'following Paul' toward his own ecclesiological ends. Return to your readings from Koester, Brown and Schüssler Fiorenza. How do you

read Luke's presentation of the early church, and his interpretation of Paul in the light of these different theories about the origins and development of the church?

21 October: Paul according to Ephesians and Colossians
Read: Ephesians and Colossians

> **Walter F. Taylor and John H. P. Reumann in *Ephesians and Colossians*, Introductions, pp. 9-25; 107-14, and employ their outlines and commentaries for your reading of the texts. Once again, it will be helpful to review your notes and/or readings from your introductory course on the New Testament.

Journal questions
How do you see Ephesians and Colossians 'following Paul'? Cite some specific examples of where you see definite points of contact and divergence with the '7 Authentic'. What does the church look like in these letters? What is the understanding of mission? Cite specific texts and discuss them as examples.

28 October: Reading Week – No Class

4 November: Paul according to 1 and 2 Timothy and Titus
Read: 1 and 2 Timothy and Titus

> Jouette M. Bassler, *1 Timothy, 2 Timothy, and Titus* (Nashville: Abingdon, 1996) and employ her outlines and commentary for your reading of the texts

> **Luise M. Schottroff, 'Oppression of Women and Hatred of Women's Liberation (1 Timothy 2.9-15)', in *Lydia's Impatient Sisters*, trans. Barbara and Martin Rumscheidt (Louisville: Westminster/John Knox Press, 1995), pp. 69-78

Journal questions
How would you characterize the way in which the PE 'follow Paul'. What are some distinctive features? Where do you see points of contact with Paul's letters? Where do you see points of divergence? How would you characterize the ecclesiology and missiology of the PE? Cite specific texts and discuss them as examples.

11 November: Paul according to the Apocryphal Legends
Read:

> **'The Acts of Paul', in *The New Testament Apocrypha*, vol. 2, ed. Wilhelm Schneemelcher, trans. R. McL. Wilson (Philadelphia: Westminster Press, 1965), pp. 322-90 (note: pp. 322-51 are a helpful introduction, and can be viewed as a supplement to MacDonald).

> Dennis R. MacDonald, *The Legend and the Apostle: The Battle for Paul in Story and Canon* (Philadelphia: Westminster Press, 1983)

Journal questions
What are some of the distinctive ways in which the *Acts of Paul* depict Paul, his vision of the church and its mission? What are the points from Paul's writings where you see a basis for these depictions? How might you describe the ecclesiology and missiology of the churches connected to these legends? How do they differ from the churches of the Pastoral Epistles?

18 November: Paul according to the Gnostics
Read:

> **'The Prayer of the Apostle', trans. Dieter Mueller, in *The Nag Hammadi Library*, James M. Robinson (ed.) (New York: HarperCollins, 1988), pp. 27-28; 'The Interpretation of Knowledge', trans. Elaine H. Pagels, in *The Nag Hammadi Library*, pp. 472-80

> Elaine Pagels, *The Gnostic Paul: Gnostic Exegesis of the Pauline Letters* (Philadelphia: Trinity Press International, 1992)

Journal questions
How do these Gnostic texts 'follow Paul'? What are their distinctive features? Where can you see them interpreting Paul? What texts or themes do they seem to be drawing on? What might they ignore? What is the church and what is its mission in Gnostic interpretations of Paul? What have you learned from this 'heresy'?

25 November: Society of Biblical Literature Meeting – No Class

2 December: Paul according to Marcion
Read:

> **Adolph von Harnack, *Marcion: The Gospel of an Alien God*, trans. John E. Steely and Lyle D. Bierma (Durham, NC: Labyrinth Press, 1990), pp. 21–92

Journal questions
How do Marcion's canon list and *Antitheses* represent an attempt to 'follow Paul'? What do you think of his interpretation? What points of contact do you see with your interpretation of Paul? What points of disagreement do you see? Cite specific examples. What is the church and what is its mission according to Marcion? What have you learned from this 'heretic'?

9 December: Will the Real Paul Please Stand Up? Will the Real Church Please Stand up?
Read:

> Bruce Bawer, *Stealing Jesus: How Fundamentalism Betrays Christianity* (New York: Three Rivers Press, 1998)

Journal questions
Bawer's vision of church and mission draw in many ways on a particular following of Paul. Where do you see this? Cite specific texts as examples. What do you think of this vision of the church and its mission? Where do you see points of contact with some of the ancient interpreters of Paul?

Journal Due at the End of Class
16 December: Final Paper Due
** denotes readings that are being placed on reserve/and or electronic reserve at the Eden-Webster Library.

Appendix 2
The 'Silenced' Women of 1 Timothy 2.8-15
A Dramatic Liturgical Reading

Deborah Krause

Woman 1: We are the silenced women of 1 Timothy.

Woman 2: Yes - you have heard him say 'Let a woman learn in silence and with all submission.'

Woman 3: ... and don't forget the part about 'I permit no woman to teach or have authority over a man.'

Woman 1: That *is* the kicker!

Woman 2: But the worst was his justification. He based it on scripture, he appealed to Genesis 2-3, to our mother, Eve.

Woman 1: Yes he called her transgressor, the deceived one. Adam bore no guilt, he said. None at all. Eve - for him the representative of all womankind - was evil, and so therefore are we!

Woman 3: Evil, Transgressors. He called us those names, and said that was why we must remain silent.

Woman 2: But we never were silent, and we aren't silent today. We're talking to you now, aren't we? And we're teaching you right now ... and some of you are men!

Woman 1: Back then we were teaching in the church. Some of us were widows. We had duties, we had responsibilities. We, he told you, were 'gossips' and 'busybodying' and 'idle, gadding about from house to house' - well, *that* was *his* perception!

Woman 3: House to house was how we practised our ministry. Some of us were widows, some were midwives, others were nurses, and others teachers and evangelists. We talked to people, we encouraged new members, we taught and preached the gospel - this is what we were doing!

Woman 2: And we were doing it well. We were effective and successful!

Woman 1: But he called us transgressors, he commanded our silence.

Woman 2: And it is like we have always been trying to say . . .

Woman 1, 2, 3 (together): You don't tell women to shut up unless they are saying something!

Woman 3: So remember our story. We're in your Bibles, in between the lines, and in the midst of all that heated rhetoric you can hear our voices.

Woman 1: We are the 'silenced' women of 1 Timothy, but don't believe everything you read!

Woman 2: Because we weren't silent, and that was his problem. We threatened his power. We challenged his definition of the church. We resisted his constraints, and we are still resisting them today. We are called and claimed by God to minister with our communities in love.

Woman 3: And we won't be silent.

Woman 1: We can't be silent!

Woman 1, 2, 3 (together): We too are the church. We too are God's people. We too have a lot to say!

Appendix 3
Paul's Flesh Become Word - A Comparison of the Citation of Scripture in 1 Corinthians 9.8-14 and 1 Timothy 5.17-18

In order for the genre of pseudepigraphy to be rhetorically successful the audience of the letter needs to be persuaded that the writing is genuine. In order to bear the authority of Paul, the letter writer's audience must be convinced that indeed the present letter comes from Paul himself (Donelson, 55-56). Such a demand for Pauline flavour requires that the letter writer represents Paul's style and mimics his idiosyncrasies, and yet this must be done without the flagrant copying of Paul's writings. Such a copying would denote direct evidence of literary borrowing, and that would reveal the presence of a precursor authoritative text, and such a situation would not have occurred to Paul. He did not understand his own writings to be at the level of scripture (*graphe*). This placed the PE writer, who likely did consider Paul's letters as sacred, authoritative writings, in a very challenging position. He had to represent them, and interpret Paul's ideas to suit his purposes, while at the same time not directly copying their content.

As the Pastoral Epistles were presented to their original intended audience, they were no doubt hailed as lost letters of the revered leader Paul. Their contents would have likely amazed the recipients for their timely handling of issues so much at stake in the recipients' communities. As the church's leadership struggled with particular opponents, and grappled with issues of governance and discipline, these letters arrived like an answer to prayer. Here, within these lines the church could gain access into the unfettered instruction of Paul. They had their answer to the question W.W.P.S.? (What would Paul say?). As the readers would hang on every line, the pseudepigrapher knew he must present Paul with the utmost care and skill. He must walk the thin line between making the letters believable in their Pauline character and yet distinct enough not to be detected as direct forgeries.

For this reason 1 Timothy, 2 Timothy and Titus represent much early church traditional material, such as hymns, confessions, doxologies and household codes, but they do not directly quote from the seven authentic letters of Paul. Within the letters, however, there are some examples of literary borrowing that can be demonstrated. This appendix takes up the demonstration of one such example. Through this demonstration one can see how the letter writer is reading and interpreting Paul's letters, and through the transformation of the Pauline text into the PE writer's text, one can detect the particular ways in which the letter writer construed Paul's own practice and beliefs toward the goal of shaping the practices of his own church.

1 Timothy 5.17-18 quotes Deuteronomy 25.4 and a Jesus logion for the purpose of establishing scriptural proof for the payment of elders who preach and teach within the church. While the writer of 1 Timothy often quotes scripture and cites tradition, this particular citation is interesting because it closely follows a similar quotation in 1 Corinthians 9.8-14. The letter writer procures a portion of Paul's deliberation from 1 Corinthians 9 regarding the rights of apostles and the limitation of individual rights for the sake of the broader community, he compresses Paul's rhetoric and asserts two of Paul's claims out of the Deuteronomy quotation and the Jesus logion, as scriptural (*graphe*) warrant for an ecclesial rule about the double compensation of elders. In this act of literary borrowing the PE writer interprets the traditions through Paul and elevates the words of Jesus, and to a certain extent the words of Paul, to the level of scripture. In this he presents a decisively different hermeneutical posture to Paul.

1 Timothy 5.17-18

> Let the elders who rule well be considered worthy of double honor, especially those who labor in teaching and preaching; for the scriptures says, 'You shall not muzzle the ox when it is treading the grain', and 'the laborer deserves his wages'. (RSV)

1 Corinthians 9.8-14

> Do I say this on human authority? Does the law not say the same? For it is written in the law of Moses, 'You shall not muzzle the ox when it is treading the grain.' Is it for the oxen that God is concerned? Does he not speak entirely for our own sake? It was written for our sake, because the plowman should plow in hope and the thresher thresh in hope of a share of the crop. If you have sown spiritual good among you, is it too much if we reap your material benefits? If others share this rightful claim upon you, do not we still more?
>
> Nevertheless we have not made use of this right but we endure anything rather than put an obstacle in the way of the gospel of Christ. Do you not know those who are employed in the temple service get their food from the temple, and those who serve at the altar share in sacrificial offerings? In the same way, the Lord

commanded that those who proclaim the gospel should get their living by the gospel. (RSV)

A comparison of the 1 Corinthians and 1 Timothy texts reveals a marked difference in the appropriation and handling of the same traditions. In 1 Corinthians 9 Paul does not merely cite Deuteronomy 25.4, but also delves into the larger context of that citation for his anthropological interpretation of the ox and the grain (alluding to Deuteronomy 24.14-15 in 1 Corinthians 9.10 and Deuteronomy 18.1-8 in 1 Corinthians 9.13). Moreover, Paul expands his application of the Deuteronomy tradition with an allusion to *Sirach* 6.9: 'Like one who plows and sows come to her and await her good fruit.' This Midrashic effort demonstrates that Paul is compelled to argue for his interpretation of Deuteronomy 25.4. This is so, because he is making a somewhat novel application of a peculiar agrarian law to the situation of compensation for those who proclaim the gospel.

In Paul's use of the various traditions about agriculture he is building a hermeneutical case that the reference to the ox is intended 'for our sake'. To this case based upon scripture traditions of both legal code and wisdom, Paul appends a 'saying of the Lord'. It is important to note that Paul does not handle the Jesus logion in the same way he does the traditions from Deuteronomy and *Sirach*. Rather, after he has made his exegetical case from the 'law of Moses', he then offers the confirmation of the Lord's saying as a kind of 'clincher' to the argument. Importantly Paul does not directly quote any known Jesus logion; however, most scholars are agreed that his summary, 'those who proclaim the gospel should make their living by the gospel' is a summary of the saying found in Q 'for the workman deserves his wages' (Lk. 10.7/Mt. 10.10).

Most significant about Paul's exegetical and hermeneutical effort in 1 Corinthians 9.8-14 is the rhetorical use he makes of the scriptural warrants for the rights of Apostles in the larger section of 1 Corinthians 9.1-27. After he has made his case based upon scripture and the Lord's saying, he then goes on to demonstrate to the Corinthians that he has never made use of his right to lodging or board among them. In this Paul elaborately establishes the tradition of the rights of Apostles, but claims that for his own pastoral practice among the Corinthians he has made an exception to his rights: 'we have not made use of this right, but we endure anything rather than put an obstacle in the way of the gospel of Christ' (1 Cor. 9.12).

The highly developed application of scripture and Jesus tradition in 1 Corinthians 9.8-14 reveals Paul's response to a charge against him in Corinth that he does not behave like a genuine apostle (1 Cor. 9.3:

'This is my defence for those who would examine me'). In this defence he holds himself up as an example of what it means to suspend one's individual rights (*exousia*) and one's individual freedom in the gospel for the good of the whole community. In this sense, Paul knits the elaborate combination of scripture exegesis and reference to the Jesus logion to his own personal example on behalf of teaching the Corinthian church how to manage their own persons, rights and freedoms in relationship to one another. Through his use of the tradition, Paul lays bare the particularities of his practices as an apostle, and deftly weaves his life into the tradition in a kind of conversation about who he is in relationship to the Corinthian church, and what it means for him to proclaim the gospel among them in the ways that he does. Through this combination of scripture exegesis and personal example Paul presents a complex hermeneutical claim that under-scores his fundamental understanding of his calling as an apostle:

> For though I am free with respect to all, I have made myself a slave to all, so that I might win more of them. To the Jews I became a Jew, in order to win Jews. To those under the law I became as one under the law (though I myself am not under the law) so that I might win those under the law. To those outside the law I became as one outside the law (though I am not free from God's law, but under Christ's law) so that I might win those outside the law. To the weak I have become weak so that I might win the weak. I have become all things to all people, that I might by all means save some. I do it all for the sake of the gospel, so that I may share in its blessings. (1 Cor. 9.19-24, NRSV)

Within the context of 1 Corinthians 9 the issue of the material compensation of apostles does not yet seem to be a crisis for Paul. He explains his practice of revoking his right to compensation as a means toward teaching the Corinthians that they should withhold their rights in Christ to eat food that has been sacrificed to idols in order to uphold those in the community for whom such a practice would have been a problem (1 Corinthians 8-10). His personal example as one who has not claimed all of his rights serves as a model for his call that the Corinthians understand that indeed 'all things are lawful', but not all things are beneficial and not all things build up (1 Cor. 10.23). On behalf of the larger community, Paul calls the Corinthians not to seek their own advantage, but that of the other (1 Cor. 10.24).

Later in Paul's relationship with the Corinthian church, however, his practice of not demanding material compensation does seem to have proposed a crisis for his leadership with the community. In the letter fragments contained in 2 Corinthians Paul responds to the pressure of those 'professional' apostles who come into the community bearing letters of recommendation (2 Cor. 3.1-2), and who, unlike Paul and his followers, expect compensation (2 Cor. 11.7-9). Here it is clear that Paul's proof of the rights of apostles to compensation that he makes in 1 Corinthians 9.8-14 was indeed held to by some leaders within the church as a legitimizing mark of an apostle. According to this group, Paul, no matter his pastoral reasons for declining his rights to compensation, demonstrated himself to be less than legitimate in his refusal of compensation for his work in preaching and teaching in the church.

In the light of this development within Paul's own ministry with the Corinthian church, the PE writer's appropriation of Deuteronomy 25.4 and the Jesus logion is particularly startling. Writing in the name of Paul the PE writer takes up the traditions Paul had combined to authorize the rights of apostles to compensation and applies them directly to an ecclesial order for the extra compensation (*diples times*) of those elders who labour in teaching and preaching in the church. Paul innovated the combination of these different traditions in order to establish the authority for a right that he did not demand. The PE writer, on the other hand, takes the combination of the Deuteronomy 25.4 and Jesus logion as a given, and offers them together as justification for a structured pay scale within an established ecclesial office (*presbuteros*).

A close look at the PE writer's appropriation of Paul's tradition is instructive of the vast differences between his and Paul's reference to the Deuteronomy text and Jesus logion. First, in 1 Timothy 5.18 the PE writer compresses Paul's elaborate apology for the use of an agrarian law in reference to the treatment of apostles into the simple citation of the Deuteronomy 25.4 text. The Pastoral Epistle letter writer is not compelled to justify the use of the tradition with reference to apostles because indeed Paul had already made that case. By the time the PE writer wrote 1 Timothy the Deuteronomy tradition had become a stock proof text for the compensation of church leaders. What was for Paul an innovative appropriation of scripture in the midst of a contextual struggle to assert his apostolic authority and teach the Corinthians about individual freedoms and corporate responsibilities had become for the PE writer a standard resource for a particular ecclesial practice.

The second difference between Paul's use of the Deuteronomy and Jesus logion traditions and that of the PE writer can be seen in the different formulae they use to introduce the traditions. In 1 Corinthians 9.9 Paul introduces the Deuteronomy text with the phrase 'it has been written [*gegraptai*] in the law of Moses'. Later in his deliberation Paul then cites the Jesus logion with the phrase: 'the Lord commanded'. Paul links his use of the Jesus logion not to the Deuteronomy text directly, but rather to Paul's illustration of those who work within the service of the temple and the sacrificial altar. Just as (*outos*) such folk receive compensation for their food from the temple and altar, so did the Lord command that those who proclaim the gospel should get their living by the gospel. Paul's reference to the Jesus tradition is not explicitly textual. Rather in his use of the verb 'commanded' (*dietaxen*), and in the lack of verbal agreement between his reference and the logion in Q (Lk. 10.7, Mt. 10.10), one could surmise that Paul was citing the tradition from memory. At the very least it is clear that Paul did not think of Deuteronomy 25.4 and the Jesus logion as the same kind of tradition. He handled the material differently, quoting the 'law' while alluding to the Lord's command. In addition he upheld these traditions as authorities for apostolic compensation, and yet personally superseded their application on behalf of his, apparently, more authoritative service of the Corinthian church. In other words, his personal practice and relationship with the Corinthians called for a contextually sensitive and vocationally lithe response to the 'law of Moses' and the 'command' of the Lord.

The PE writer, in contrast to Paul, cites the Deuteronomy 25.4 tradition and the Jesus logion in the same verse. They are introduced at once with the formula 'for it is written', (*legei gar he graphe*), and coordinated to this formula with an 'and' (*kai*) conjunction. In this introduction the PE writer not only reveals his assessment of both Torah and Jesus tradition as 'scripture' (something Paul never does), but he also applies them directly and without irony to the justification of a practice that Paul had denied himself. In a sense, the PE writer uses the Pauline combination and exposition of the traditions in order to establish additional rights to pastoral compensation that Paul had originally resisted. The entire appropriation focuses on the text of Paul's use of the traditions without any imagination regarding their application. The hermeneutical approach to scripture and authoritative tradition is markedly different between the two letters. While the letters both cite the same traditions, they come to mean entirely different things, and have entirely different applications.

Paul's letters are filled with his personal example. He draws on his suffering and challenges as an apostle as paranetic material for his congregations. While the writer of 1 Timothy seeks to mimic Paul's style of writing, and even in the case of 1 Timothy 5.18 cites Paul's use of tradition in 1 Corinthians 9.8-14, he does not imitate his pastoral practice or application of tradition and authority. In a sense, Paul's citation of the tradition had been completely embodied. His own personal situation, and contextual struggle as an apostle, are bound up in his reference to Deuteronomy 25.4 and the Jesus logion. He is not citing these traditions as proof texts to justify his own practice, but is rather setting up the complex reality of what his rights are in comparison to what his actual practices are within the Corinthian community. The entire appropriation demonstrates the contextual nature of his understanding of the tradition and its authority, and his own authority as an apostle. These things are for Paul very much under negotiation with the Corinthians. As becomes clear in 2 Corinthians the matters of apostolic authority and compensation become a central part of a debate between Paul and the 'super apostles' who challenge his authority and teaching within the church (2 Corinthians 10-11). In 1 Corinthians 9.8-14 Paul uses all aspects of the tradition he has at hand (Torah and Jesus tradition) and his own personal example to compel the Corinthians to see his plight and to appreciate his ministry among them.

The PE writer cites the traditions in an entirely different way to Paul. In his hermeneutic the words on the page are of the same authority, namely the Deuteronomy and Jesus traditions are both understood as 'scripture' (*graphe*). Moreover the entire drama of Paul's personal example is absent from the PE writer's presentation of the issue. Gone is Paul's personal example of declining his rights to apostolic privilege on behalf of the greater good of the community. Gone is the impetus to teach the church through the intersection of Paul's personal example and the different authoritative traditions of Deuteronomy and the Lord's saying. In the place of these elements the references to Deuteronomy 25.4 and the Jesus logion stand as proofs for the practice of doubly compensating preaching and teaching elders within the church. Importantly in this transformation the notion of using the traditions to support the practice of paying apostles is assumed, and the traditions now stand to support the extra compensation of a select few elders who labour in teaching and preaching within the church.

The differences between the appropriation of Deuteronomy 25.4 and the Jesus logion in 1 Corinthians 9.8-14 and 1 Timothy 5.18 reveal the marked differences between the two letters, and the nature of the understanding of the ecclesia at work within the letters. In 1 Corinthians Paul is engaged in a personal struggle to assert his apostolic authority among the Corinthians. He is working hard in the letter to engage them through a variety of means. He cannot assume anything about his office or title in relationship to them. Rather, he has to apologize for the particularities of his practice as an apostle among them, and he uses the differences in practice as a means to instruct the Corinthians on how they might be a community who put the needs of the group over the rights of individuals. In 1 Timothy the letter writer employs tradition that Paul had engaged with his own personal example in order to establish the particular rights and functions of a given office in the church (the office of elder). In this letter the formation of the church is established, Paul's authority is a given. The very things that had been under negotiation within the Corinthian correspondence are in fact the sound and right teaching upon which the church, its offices and practices are established. Paul is an apostle with great authority, and those who preach and teach are indeed afforded a living by the church, and in fact are lobbying for a greater share in the church's financial support.

Throughout the seven uncontested letters Paul urges the members of his churches to 'imitate' him as he imitates Christ. He uses his personal example as a means of teaching his churches how it is they are to be in relationship with one another and with God through Jesus Christ. His sufferings and his struggles as an apostle supply him with material by which he can teach his churches about the life of the gospel and the nature of the church. In 1 Timothy 5.17-18 the PE writer imitates Paul's writing in 1 Corinthians 9.8-14. He borrows Paul's appropriation of the traditions from Deuteronomy 25.4 and the Jesus logion in order to establish an ecclesial practice of compensating teaching and preaching elders. This imitation reflects the letter writer's knowledge of the text of 1 Corinthians in terms of the traditional content, but seems to miss the imitation of Paul's personal example. In this sense, the letters of Paul (at least 1 Corinthians) seem to have become a kind of scripture (*graphe*) for the letter writer. While he cannot directly copy Paul's earlier writings in his use of pseudepigrapha, he must sound enough like Paul and use Paul's traditions in such a way that his letters will ring true for their audience. In this case he engages Paul's language at the level of text, as proof. In so doing, however, he misunderstands the nature of Paul's personal example, and directs the teaching of 1 Corinthians into a piece of ecclesial order. In this Paul's authority has shifted from the imitation of his personal example and suffering as he imitates Christ, into a sense of the authority of his words within his letters.

The phenomenon of imitation at work in 1 Timothy 5.17-18 underscores the distance between the PE writer and the historical Paul. First, it underscores the historical difference. It seems highly unlikely that even years later in his ministry Paul would so woodenly refer to his own earlier argument from Deuteromony 25.4 and the Jesus logion, and yet so completely reverse the application of the original teaching. In this sense, the literary effort of 1 Timothy 5.17-18 represents a misquotation and misapplication of the 1 Corinthians material, and it makes no sense that Paul would refer to himself and his teaching in this way. Second, it underscores hermeneutical difference. A comparison of the texts reveals markedly different sensibilities about the nature of the tradition and how it bears its authority. For Paul, this is a deeply personal venture. He engages the tradition in relationship to his own practice of ministry, and establishes thereby a call for his church to live lithely in response to the law, and to hold the good of the community as a priority over the particular rights and privileges conferred by the tradition. For the PE writer, the tradition represents a base upon which he can advocate and adjudicate certain aspects of the church's order. Far from a personal engagement, the PE writer takes the combination of the Deuteronomy and Jesus logion traditions found in 1 Corinthians and crafts them as a rule. Importantly, the PE writer does not apply the rule mechanically to his community, rather he uses it as a base to argue for the expansion of clergy rights to compensation over what had been the general practice (*double* honour, as opposed to honour). In this sense, his application of the traditions is no less creative than Paul's, but his appropriation of the traditions derives from a different sense of what the authoritative tradition is and how he stands in relationship to it. The historical and hermeneutical differences between the texts in 1 Corinthians and 1 Timothy represent very different understandings of ministry and very different understandings of the church.

In his study of the phenomenon of imitation within Renaissance poetry, Thomas M. Greene notes that attempts to imitate the writing of an author 'contain by definition a revivalist initiative, a gesture that signals the intent to reanimate an earlier text or texts' (37). In his work *Echoes of Scripture in the Letters of Paul*, Richard Hays notes that Greene's discussion of imitation applies well to the phenomenon of the PE (Hays, 175). While Hays does not discuss the appropriation of 1 Corinthians 9.8-14 in 1 Timothy 5.17-18 he does note that Greene's category of 'sacramental imitation' applies most fully to the reanimation of Paul in the Pastorals. Greene's description of this category of appropriation does seem to capture the dynamic of the imitation of Paul's words from 1 Corinthians in 1 Timothy. According to Greene, in sacramental imitation 'the model or subtext is perceived as a fixed object on the far side of an abyss, beyond alteration, beyond criticism, a sacred original' (Greene, 38). As Jürgen Roloff has noted about the Pastoral Epistles in general, the extent of the authority of Paul's revelation in his churches caused the crisis that necessitated the pseudepigraphical representation of Paul (Roloff, 379). In other words, no one could assume Paul's place, but rather his voice had to be extended and imitated for the church to receive new authoritative teaching. The irony of this posture toward Paul and his authority, however, ultimately yielded writings, of which 1 Timothy is an example, that imitated Paul, and yet somehow misrepresented his positions. According to Greene, such a dynamic is a phenomenon of sacramental imitation. He notes that seeing the model text (in this case 1 Cor. 9.8-14) as a 'great original' actually asserts the presence of a false archetype. As such, sacramental imitation may copy, or attempt to represent the original, but paradoxically it cannot attain genuine contact with the original (Greene, 39).

In a different contemporary theory about textual appropriations Harold Bloom offers a compelling model through which to consider the relationship between the PE writer and Paul. In his work *The Anxiety of Influence* he outlines a theory about poets and their precursors that connects in many ways to the relationship between the PE writer and Paul. According to Bloom strong poets of creative genius are able to overcome the sense of dread posed by the presence and work of those poets who precede them. They are able to honour the tradition, incorporate it into their own work, and yet still carve out a new space for themselves. Weak poets, on the other hand, do not have this capability. They rewrite the work of their precursors unwittingly and cannot appropriate their work creatively to say something new. Rather, Bloom argues, such weak poets are victims, and 'pseudo-exegetes who make writings into scriptures' (Bloom, 35).

In many ways the writer of 1 Timothy is postured toward Paul as a weak poet. Paul understood his entire revelation in deeply personal terms. Now the church is forced to continue on in his absence. As Paul had used letters to stand in for his presence with his churches, now the PE writer uses the letter in Paul's name to fill in for the Apostle's permanent absence and to claim his authority. Through this form of imitation, however, the PE writer does not merely imitate Paul, but powerfully appropriates him and his language toward a vision of the church and its offices that Paul never shared. As an imitator we might disparage the PE writer for his lack of originality. As one who directed Paul's language toward a new context, however, he employed imitation with innovation. His imitation of Paul may not be artful, but it has tremendous rhetorical power. It manages, in the case of 1 Timothy 5.17-18, at once to honour the legacy of Paul, yet completely to reinvent his words. The PE writer through his imitation of the tradition managed to erase Paul's personal pastoral practice while establishing a general clerical model.

Bibliography

Aune, David E., *Prophecy in Earliest Christianity and the Ancient Mediterranean World* (Grand Rapids: Eerdmans, 1983).

Bahktin, M. M., *The Dialogic Imagination, Four Essays by M. M. Bahktin*, ed. and trans M. Holquist (Austin: University of Texas Press, 1988).

Barr, James, *Holy Scripture: Canon, Authority, Criticism* (Philadelphia: Westminster Press, 1983).

Bassler, Jouette M., 'The Widow's Tale: A Fresh Look at 1 Timothy 5.3-16', *Journal of Biblical Literature* 103 (1984), pp. 23-41.

——*1 Timothy, 2 Timothy, and Titus* (Nashville: Abingdon, 1996).

Bauer, Walter, *Orthodoxy and Heresy in Earliest Christianity*, trans. Philadelphia Seminar on Christian Origins (Philadelphia: Fortress, 1971).

Baur, F. C. *Die sogenannten Pastoralbriefe des Apostles Paulus aufs neue kritisch untersucht* (Stuttgart and Tübingen: J. G. Cotta, 1835).

——*The Church History of the First Three Centuries*, vol. I, trans. Allan Menzies (London and Edinburgh: Williams & Norgate, 1878).

Bloom, Harold, *The Anxiety of Influence: A Theory of Poetry* (London/New York: Oxford University Press, 1975).

Campenhausen, Hans von, *The Formation of the Christian Bible*, trans. J. A. Baker (Philadelphia: Fortress Press, 1972).

Collins, Patricia Hill, *Black Feminist Thought: Knowledge, Consciousness, and the Politics of Empowerment*, 2nd edn (London/New York: Routledge, 2000).

Collins, Raymond, *1 & 2 Timothy and Titus* (Louisville and London: Westminster/John Knox Press, 2002).

Davis, Stevan L., *The Revolt of the Widows: The Social World of the Apocryphal Acts* (Carbondale and Edwardsville: Southern Illinois University Press, 1980).

Deissmann, Adolf, *Light from the Ancient East: The New Testament Illustrated by Recently Discovered Texts of the Graeco-Roman World*, trans. Lionel R. M. Strachan (New York: George H. Doran Co., 1927).

Dibelius, Martin and Conzelmann, Hans, *The Pastoral Epistles*, trans. Philip Buttolph and Adele Yarbro (Philadelphia: Fortress, 1972).

Donelson, Lewis, *Pseudepigraphy and Ethical Argument in the Pastoral Epistles* (Tübingen: Mohr–Siebeck, 1986).

——*Colossians, Ephesians, 1 and 2 Timothy, and Titus* (Louisville: Westminster/John Knox Press, 1996).

Doniger, Wendy, *The Implied Spider: Politics and Theology in Myth* (New York: Columbia University Press, 1998).

Duff, Jeremy, 'P46 and the Pastorals: A Misleading Comparison', *New Testament Studies* 44 (1988), pp. 578-90.

Dunn, James D. G., 'The First and Second Letters to Timothy and the Letter to Titus', in *The New Interpreter's Bible*, vol. XI (Nashville: Abingdon, 2000), pp. 775-880.

Fewell, Danna Nolen and David Gunn, *Gender, Power, and Promise: The subject of the Bible's first story*. (Nashville: Abingdon, 1993).

Goss, Robert, *Jesus Acted Up: A Gay and Lesbian Manifesto* (New York: HarperCollins, 1993).

Green, Thomas M., *The Light of Troy: Imitation and Discovery in Renaissance Poetry* (New Haven: Yale University Press, 1986).

Harnack, Adolf von, *What is Christianity?*, trans. Thomas Bailey Sanders (New York: Putnam, 1901).

Hays, Richard B., *Echoes of Scripture in the Letters of Paul* (New Haven: Yale University Press, 1989).

Holmes, J. M., *Text in a Whirlwind: A Critique of Four Exegetical Devices at 1 Timothy 2.9-15* (Sheffield: Sheffield Academic Press, 2000).

Kidd, Reggie M., *Wealth and Beneficence in the Pastoral Epistles* (Atlanta: Scholars Press, 1990).

Koester, Helmut, 'Gnomai Diáphorai: The Origin and Nature of Diversification in Early Christianity', *Harvard Theological Review* 58 (1965), pp. 279-318.

Krause, Deborah and Timothy K. Beal, 'Higher Critics on Late Texts: Reading Biblical Scholarship After the Holocaust', in Tod Linafelt (ed.), *A Shadow of Glory: Reading the New Testament After the Holocaust* (London/New York: Routledge, 2002).

Lefkowitz, Mary and Maureen B. Fant, *Women's Life in Greece and Rome* (Baltimore: Johns Hopkins University Press, 1982).

Lipps, Hermann Von, *Glaube, Gemeinde, Amt: zum Verständnis die Ordination in die Pastoralbriefen* (Göttingen: Vandenhoeck & Ruprecht, 1979).

Lyotard, Jean-François, *The Postmodern Explained*, trans. Don Barry *et al.* (Minneapolis: University of Minnesota Press, 1992).

MacDonald, Dennis R., *The Legend and the Apostle: The Battle for Paul in Story and Canon* (Philadelphia: Westminster, 1983).

Malherbe, Abraham J., *Moral Exhortation, A Greco-Roman Sourcebook* (Philadelphia: Westminster Press, 1986).

Miller, James D., *The Pastoral Epistles as Composite Documents* (Cambridge: Cambridge University Press, 1997).

Pagels, Elaine, *The Gnostic Gospels* (New York: Random House, 1979).

——*Adam, Eve, and the Serpent* (New York: Random House, 1988).

——*The Gnostic Paul: Gnostic Exegesis of the Pauline Letters* (Philadelphia: Trinity, 1975, 1992).

Pollitt, Katha, 'God Changes Everything', *The Nation*, 274, 1 April 2002, p. 10.

Quinn, Jereme and William C. Wacker, *The First and Second Letters to Timothy* (Grand Rapids: Eerdmans, 2000).

Rawls, Philip, 'House Candidate uses Bible to Defend Southern Slavery', Associated Press, 5 May 1996.

Roberts, Alexander and James Donaldson, *Ante-Nicean Fathers: The Writings of the Fathers Down to 325 AD*, 10 vols (Peabody, MA: Hendrickson, 1994).

Roloff, Jürgen, *Der Erste Brief an Timotheus* (Zurich: Benziger Verlag, 1988).

Schneemelcher, Wilhelm, *The New Testament Apocrypha*, 2 vols, trans. R. McL. Wilson (Louisville: Westminster/John Knox Press, 1991-92).

Schottroff, Luise M., 'Oppression of Women and Hatred of Women's Liberation', in *Lydia's Impatient Sisters: A Feminist Social History of Early Christianity* (Louisville: Westminister/John Knox, 1995), pp. 69-78.

Schüssler Fiorenza, Elisabeth, *In Memory of Her: A Feminist-Theological Reconstruction of Christian Origins* (New York: Crossroad, 1983).

——*Wisdom Ways: Introducing Feminist Biblical Interpretation* (Maryknoll: Orbis, 2001).

Stählin, Gustav, in *Theological Dictionary of New Testament*, ed. Gerhard Friedrich, trans. Geoffrey W. Bromiley, vol. IX (Grand Rapids: Eerdmans, 1974).

Stanton, Elizabeth Cady and the Revising Committee, *The Woman's Bible* (New York: European Publishing Co., 1898).

Stowers, Stanley K., *Letter Writing in Greco-Roman Antiquity* (Philadelphia: Westminster Press, 1986).

Thurston, Bonnie Bowman, *The Widows: A Women's Ministry in the Early Church* (Minneapolis: Fortress Press, 1989).

Verner, David C., *The Household of God: The Social World of the Pastoral Epistles* (Chico, CA: Scholars Press, 1983).

Vice, Sue, *Introducing Bakhtin* (Manchester: Manchester University Press, 1997).

Lexica

Bauer, Walter, William Arndt, F. W. Gingrich, and Frederick W. Danker, *A Greek-English Lexicon of the New Testament and Other Early Christian Literature* (Chicago and London: The University of Chicago Press, 1979).

Liddell, Henry George and Robert Scott, *A Greek-English Lexicon* (New York: American Book Company, 1897).

Ecclesiastical Documents

'The Baptist Faith and Message', Southern Baptist Convention (adopted 14 June, 2000). (http://www.sbc.net/bfm/default.asp).

'Women in the Church: Scriptural Principles and Ecclesial Practice', A Report of the Commission on Theology and Church Relations of the Lutheran Church, Missouri Synod, September 1985 (http://www.lcms.org/ctcr/docs/women-01.html).

INDEXES

INDEX OF REFERENCES

OLD TESTAMENT

OTHER EARLY CHRISTIAN WRITINGS

INDEX OF AUTHORS